Distinctively
Christian

A Christ-centered Worldview Approach
to Elementary Ministry

Milton V. Uecker Ed.D and Anne Marie Gosnell M.Ed.

An Engaged Schools Initiative Resource

Distinctively Christian:
A Christ-centered Worldview Approach to Elementary Ministry

Published by Wheaton Press
Wheaton, Illinois
www.WheatonPress.com

ISBN-10: 1950258327
ISBN-13: 978-1-950258-32-1 (WheatonPress.com)

1. Early Childhood Education 2. Education – Teaching. 3. Christian Education. 4. Education – Philosophy. 5. Education & Reference

Go to www.WheatonPress.com to learn about additional resources.

What people are saying about Distinctively Christian

A Christ-centered Worldview Approach to Elementary Ministry

In *Distinctively Christian*, Uecker and Gosnell offer us a wealth of information and strategies to help elementary Bible teachers use their teaching time to lay the foundation for the development of a relationship with Jesus. I appreciate the emphasis on cultivating a Christian worldview while children are still young and tender. After reading this book, I know it will be a valuable resource that I will use often in my teaching and curriculum writing.

Ellen Nikkel
Bible teacher and Curriculum Writer
Released-time Christian Education

Distinctively Christian: A Christ-centered Worldview Approach to Elementary Ministry is a thorough and enlightening description of how to think through, set up, and plan transformational Christian learning for upper elementary spiritual development. Each chapter provides researched and Scripture-based practical best practices for designing curriculum for those precious children who are often overlooked when churches plan Christian education. The content of each chapter is full of applicable information for planning curriculum for all ages. Additionally, each chapter provides helpful "Reflect and Respond" prompts that anchor distinctive precepts. I loved the Christian worldview chapters that are full of overarching insights and other resources that provide foundational depth.

Richard Van Yperen
Former Curriculum Director, Eastern Christian School, North Haledon, NJ
Author: *A Complete Guide to Godly Wisdom:*
17 Wisdom Precepts from the Perfect Father Proverbs

I know Dr. Uecker as a scholar, professor, dean, speaker, author, and mentor. I have often wished he would download all of his wisdom and passion for Jesus and Jesus' little ones. And now, he has done just that. This book is a practical manual that is essential for every Christian elementary program. Dr. Uecker, the scholar, connects the reader with great authors and stories. Dr. Uecker, the professor, filters everything through the nature of the learner. Dr. Uecker, the educator and family man, makes everything practical and easy to follow. And Dr, Uecker, the child of God, permeates everything with the grace of Jesus while pointing out pitfalls that will dilute or undermine the Gospel. I have already used this book to reestablish our school's mission for discipleship as well as developing PD to equip our teachers.

Nathan Johnson, Ed.D.
Charleston Bilingual Academy
Headmaster

Distinctively Christian challenges ministries to do more than teach Bible stories. The book's emphasis on a missional framework provides the "why, what, and how" required to form the foundational beliefs of a Christian worldview among its students. With its primary focus on the Gospel of Jesus Christ, Uecker and Gosnell, based upon their decades of wisdom and experience, offer a practical guide on how to bring spiritual formation to the forefront of a ministry to children. I'd love to see this invaluable guidebook in the hands of workers on my own staff and include the book's insights, like the importance of a living curriculum and parent involvement, during the training of ministry volunteers.

Dustin Ventura
Local Director of Child Evangelism Fellowship of SC Inc.
Greater Pee Dee Chapter, www.cefgpd.org

The Authors

Anne Marie Gosnell is a Bible Teacher and Bible curriculum writer with more than 30 years of experience. Anne Marie holds a B.S. in early childhood education and an MEd. in curriculum and instruction and is the author of seven books. She has created Bible object lessons and taught children about Jesus at churches, camps, Christian schools, and conferences. She is the founder of the Bible Creative Conference and FutureFlyingSaucers Resources, where she helps busy parents and church leaders teach fun, flexible, multi-age, budget-friendly Bible object lessons that enhance the spiritual growth of children. She is the family minister at her church and lives with her husband and three children in South Carolina.

Dr. Milton Uecker is a professor emeritus in the College of Education at Columbia International University in South Carolina. Prior to joining the faculty of CIU in 1995, Dr. Uecker served as an associate professor at Regent University in Virginia Beach where he directed the early childhood program. Prior to moving into higher education, he was a missionary teacher in Korea and an elementary principal and early childhood program director in Austin, TX, and Norfolk, VA. He received an M.Ed. in curriculum and instruction from the University of Texas (1975) and an Ed.D. in curriculum with an emphasis in early childhood from the University of Virginia (1989). Though retired, he continues to speak at conferences on topics related to early education and the philosophical foundations for education. He has recently authored and edited a series of books on a distinctively Christian, Christ-centered approach to early childhood education. He and his wife Linda live in South Carolina.

Acknowledgments

Dr. Connie Mitchell, dean of the College of Education at Columbia International University, for her collaboration in designing the model for a curriculum framework and the professional development seminars that followed.

Dr. Martha MacCullough, who, upon reading *Distinctively Christian: A Christ-centered Approach to Early Childhood Spiritual Development,* encouraged me to share the book with churches for application within its children's ministry to young children. It is that encouragement and the support of Wheaton Press that resulted in this elementary ministry edition.

The faithful teachers of the Progress of Redemption and Bible for Teachers courses across several generations of students at Columbia International University—Robertson McQuilkin, James M. "Buck" Hatch, Jack Layman, Mary Faith Phillips, and Anita Cooper.

Dedication

To my husband **Eric** for telling me, "Hey, maybe some other Bible teachers might need your Bible lessons!" Thank you for being my cheerleader, editor, critic, and the spiritual leader of our home. And to my children, Roy, Faith, and Leah Gosnell, who are the funniest, most wonderful kids in South Carolina!

To my wife **Linda** for her insights, encouragement, and support throughout my years of ministry and during the writing of the Distinctively Christian series, and to our sons and their wives, who are now "diligently teaching" their children and my grandchildren.

Joel and Caron Uecker
Audrey Anneliese
Meredith Violet

Josh and Alexia Uecker
Kate Angela
Hope Elizabeth
Caleb Josh

Jeremy and Elisabeth Uecker
Dorothy Anne
Sally Louise
Virginia Simpson
William Fritz

Contents

Knowledge, Skills, and Dispositions Related to a Christ-centered Worldview Approach to Elementary Ministry

Developing Focus Through an Elementary Ministry's Missional Framework

Foreword

What a joy to read this book written by my former colleague at Columbia International University, Milt Uecker, and Anne Marie Gosnell, a graduate student in my Teaching Bible course. Throughout this book, they challenge us to join them in the battle for the hearts and minds of youth. It represents the authors' lifetime of personal experiences through creating a paradigm to inspire others to cultivate their own journey toward a distinctively Christian education program.

This book provides program leaders with a "toolbox" full of selective power tools and the instruction manual on how to use them to build a ministry program for third-fifth grades.

Mining for gold is hard work! But you will never find and own the beauty of the gold nugget without the work necessary to capture it. So, when you read this book, you need to think deeply, devote yourself to study, think creatively, collaborate with other team members, and pray fervently. The "gold" is worth it.

Working together, Uecker and Gosnell transport us into the world of the heart and mind of a typical third-fifth-grade student. Blending science and the biblical nature of the learner, they analyze the major needs, interests, and cognitive abilities of the child. They give instruction on how to nurture solid spiritual formation at this specific stage of their development. We must know the mission and know our audience before we can effectively build the biblical worldview curriculum.

After establishing a foundational understanding of faith development, the importance of a "living curriculum" is explained in chapter two. I was moved to tears as I read this chapter. Here is a sample…

> *The living curriculum is life within a ministry community where teachers acknowledge God's presence, present worldview truths and character standards established by God and found in the Bible, and where children are viewed as image-bearers who are uniquely and wonderfully made.*
>
> *Children read their teachers long before they can read a book, and they continue to watch parents and teachers throughout childhood.*

The book painstakingly defines worldview and elaborates on the importance of continually transforming our understanding through the perspective of a Christ-centered worldview – despite the world's attempt to form us into its mold. Chapters 3-6 effectively interpret the four major worldview questions into the world of the child's perspective. The discussion of worldview concludes with practical examples of how to lead students to confirm their biblical worldview by putting it into real-life settings. The amount of wisdom and expertise presented in these four chapters is priceless! Read these chapters well! They are giving away gold here!

The mastery of one's worldview is powerless without understanding the plot of Scripture and the motif of God's redemptive narrative.[1] Chapter 7 demonstrates the necessity of presenting the story of redemption through a chronological overview of major stories in the Bible. The *"scarlet thread"* progressively shows Christ as our perfect redeemer and rabbi through His life, death, and resurrection. Our mission is to equip students to reflect Christ in and through every area of their lives. This should be the culmination of every ministry program.

Finally, the concluding chapters convey a detailed process whereby ministry directors can formulate a mission statement for their children's program. Uecker guides program directors/teachers like a coach delivering practical steps and questions that reveal the essentials to incorporate in the mission statement. Then, he unfolds how to move from mission and vision statements to create desired student outcomes.

He states that "The mission provides an initial overview of what the program will strive to accomplish." The vision statement expands upon the mission statement by answering the question related to the "why and what" in greater detail. Finally, the student outcomes break down the vision into statements of what the children must know, become, and choose to do (many outcomes are observable and others are not). More importantly, he includes the biblical rationale for writing a mission statement. This process is enriched with specific examples of mission and vision statements, outcomes, and curriculum frameworks.

As a carpenter would never go to work without a toolbox full of the correct tools for the job, program leaders and teachers should select the correct tools for the job and learn how to use them. Dr. Uecker and Anne Marie Gosnell have gifted us with a toolbox full of *power* tools and a manual on how to use them. I encourage you to open the toolbox, read the manual, and experience the wisdom found in this book.

Anita J Cooper, Ph.D.
Columbia International University
College of Arts and Sciences
Director of Bible Teaching Major

Him we proclaim, warning everyone and teaching everyone with all wisdom, that we may present everyone mature in Christ. For this I toil, struggling with all His energy that He powerfully works within me.

Colossians 1:28-29 (ESV)

Preface

What we have heard and learned—
that which our ancestors have told us—
we will not hide from their descendants.
We will tell the next generation
about the LORD's praiseworthy acts,
about His strength and the amazing things He has done.
He established a rule in Jacob;
he set up a law in Israel.
He commanded our ancestors
to make His deeds known to their descendants,
so that the next generation, children yet to be born,
might know about them.
They will grow up and tell their descendants about them.
Then they will place their confidence in God.
They will not forget the works of God,
and they will obey His commands.

Psalm 78: 3-7 (NET)

We have a purpose.

We are telling the "next generation about the Lord's praiseworthy acts and about His strength and the amazing things He has done."

We have been given a mission.

We have a dream wherein the next generation places its confidence in God, does not forget God's works, obeys Him, and then, in turn, grows up testifying their faith in Him to the next generation.

God's Word is the revelation of God, His thoughts, desires, and purposes. It is His voice assuring us of His love and will for us. It is His desire that every man, woman, and child be redeemed in Christ, transformed, and then sent on a mission. His general calling as seen in Matthew 28:18-29 (referred to as the Great Commission) is general in the sense that it is the task given every believer. We have also been given gifts (1 Cor. 1:4-11) and abilities that are tailored for a specific vocational calling, a calling that often includes a heart for a specific place or people group. Many of you, like me, have been called to teach and disciple within the context of a Christian school or a ministry within the local church and even more specifically placed into classrooms or programs where children are the "people group."

This book is written with upper elementary (grades 3-5) students in mind. We are not called to teach a curriculum or take center stage within a classroom. We are called to reach, teach, and disciple children. The focus must be centered on Jesus and the written Word and then be directed to the students. The Great Commandment challenges followers of Jesus to love God and love others. We first love God and then the others that He places on the path before us. If you are reading this book, then the assumption is that your path is filled with children.

This book will present a mission and vision for this rising generation. More specifically, its focus is on the development of a Christ-centered biblical worldview during a time when there is warfare, and "...the weapons of our warfare are not human weapons but are made powerful by God for tearing down strongholds" (2 Corinthians 10:4b NET). We, like those before us, must equip children with the truth in that the battle is between conflicting worldviews and the need to bring thoughts captive and obedient to Christ. We are tasked with the need to first teach the Word (truth), lead them to Christ, and then equip (disciple) and prepare children to "tear down arguments and every arrogant obstacle that is raised up against the knowledge of God" (2 Cor. 10:5a NET).

Psalm 139:3 says that God is "intimately acquainted with all our ways," and it is this knowledge that allows Him to know us as individuals and as a result meet each of our needs. If we are to be effective ministers and teachers, we too must know those we teach. The transformational process is grounded in relationships, and trustworthy relationships grounded in knowledge opens the door to Jesus.

There are developmental, or normative, characteristics that are true of most children (ages 8-11) and serve as a helpful introduction to their ways.[2] These commonalities, however, should only be viewed as a starting point since each student is growing according to their own timeline, and as they mature, they are also shaped by their individual temperaments, personalities, talents, gifts, cultural backgrounds, and past and present experiences. Jesus knew the nature and needs of people, but He also knew people as individuals, and because of this, He met them and spoke to them in accordance with who they were and what they needed. He did not apply a "one size fits all" approach. Even though instruction may most often occur within a group context, it must also be individually directed. Our message is the same, but our teaching must be directed by and empowered by the Holy Spirit and, by nature, be relational and personal.

The means or curriculum whereby a ministry can accomplish this end is overviewed in chapters 1-7 (section one). Section two (chapters 8-9) will then guide program directors through the process of creating a ministry framework whereby the mission, vision, and outcomes of its program can be clarified and form its own mission-based foundation for curriculum. Finally, the steps involved in developing the means whereby outcomes, drawn from the vision, can be assessed will also be outlined.

Part One

Knowledge, Skills, and Dispositions Related to a Christ-centered Worldview Approach to Elementary Ministry

Chapter One

Faith Development

"Hear, O Israel! The Lord is our God, the Lord is one! ⁵ You shall love the Lord your God with all your heart and with all your soul and with all your might. ⁶ These words, which I am commanding you today, shall be on your heart. ⁷ You shall teach them diligently to your sons and shall talk of them when you sit in your house and when you walk by the way and when you lie down and when you rise up. ⁸ You shall bind them as a sign on your hand and they shall be as [b]frontals [c]on your forehead. ⁹ You shall write them on the doorposts of your house and on your gates."

Deuteronomy 6:4-9

"You will keep this practice forever as a statute for yourselves and your descendants. Thus, when you have entered the land which the Lord will give you as He promised, you must observe this rite. ²⁶ When your children ask you, 'What does this rite of yours mean?' you will reply, 'It is the Passover sacrifice for the Lord, who passed over the houses of the Israelites in Egypt; when He struck down the Egyptians, He delivered our houses.'"

Exodus 12:24-27a (NIV)

Faith development is related to the cognitive, social, and moral developmental domains.[3] In each case, growth in one area impacts the others. For curriculum to be most effective, it must be grounded in an understanding of the process of faith development and its implications for instruction.

James Fowler has identified six stages in the development of faith, two of which impact the elementary years. Fowler believes that varying aspects of faith, including a person's relationships with others, view of reality, ways of responding to authority, and cognitive understanding change with time.[4] Appendix A presents an overview of and relationships between the social, cognitive, moral, and faith developmental stages. When discussing faith, Fowler is not referring to Christian faith or any particular religious belief, but rather, the system of relating to "knowing or construing by which persons apprehend themselves as related to the transcendent...." (5). Fowler views faith as multifaceted. It is composed of one's system of thought or worldview and the ability to take another's perspective.

Faith, according to Fowler, includes positions on moral issues along with a system for making moral decisions. It is also related to an understanding of what determines the limits to one's "community of faith"; a relationship to authority, reasoning strategies, and response to symbols are also facets of faith.[5] These dimensions, though seemingly complex, are identifiable with aspects of social, cognitive, and moral development.

Primal Faith

As previously discussed in the early childhood edition of *Distinctively Christian,* Fowler identifies the first stage (stage zero) as **primal faith.**[6] This is fundamental to all faith and aligns with Erickson's views on the formation of trust.[7] The Greek word for "trust" is the idea or word most closely aligned with and translated as "faith" in English, and it is during this time, birth to age 2, that initial trust is established through the nurture of and relationship to primary caregivers. Without this foundation, the ability to trust is jeopardized in all areas of life. It is important to realize you may have students that, due to life's circumstances (chronic stressors), may not have experienced a nurturing environment and, therefore, not have the trust needed to move forward. These students' primary needs will center on relationships within a loving and caring community. Nurturing will be more important than teaching.

Intuitive-projective Faith

Intuitive-projective faith (stage one), because of its characteristics, can also be referred to as impressionistic faith. The biblical concept of teaching in Deut. 6:4 is related to establishing a deep impression. The impressions would not come through formal teaching, but rather through firsthand experiences throughout the day. It is the impact or impressions of these experiences on the mind and emotions that form the "deep and lasting images" or symbols that are the basis of a given faith. Cognitively, these might be referred to as the "frames" for one's faith.[8] Even though this stage would align most directly with early childhood, one never ceases to learn from the emotions and information tied to positive experiences. These experiences need to continue as students move into an elementary ministry, especially during third and fourth grade, in that many children this age are still dependent on concrete or sensorial experiences if learning is to be meaningful.

The faith frames created within a home or classroom are remembered (Proverbs 22:6) and link the security that accompanies a frame (repeated experiences with the same context) with the safety found within a relationship with God. Teachers and parents should not view ritual as a negative or meaningless exercise. For children, rituals are dynamic experiences, especially those related to holiday celebrations. It is through the repeated activities of faith that the abstract becomes real.

Holidays are motivational learning tools. A young person's attention is given over to each special, or "holy," day. Every symbol is a reminder of the day, and with each symbol, there is a memory and meaning. This grows not only out of the motivation attached to the day but also to the experiential nature of celebrations. These celebrations involve all the senses and are repeated throughout the formative years. Even as adults, the memories of celebrations remain clear. God designed children, and He knows their primary learning style and its relationship to faith formation.

God built upon this when He instructed His people on how to teach. Passover is an example of the use of celebration and its relationship to impressionistic faith. God told His people to establish a Passover celebration as a permanent ordinance and as a memorial "throughout your generations" (Exodus 12:14). Each aspect of the celebration was linked to the story of God's power and faithfulness to His promise to

Israel. "And it will come about when your children will say to you, 'What does this rite mean to you?' that you shall say..." (Exodus 13:26).

> Celebrations set the stage for story, and story involves both concept and emotion (the heart).

Celebrations should occur within individual classrooms and special celebration gatherings where the children's ministry community gathers for a special worship assembly or chapel. As an example, Appendix C provides examples of impressionistic worship assemblies related to Advent.

Programs may want to select additional days to be celebrated. Consider possibilities throughout the liturgical and national calendar along with the truths that might be included during the days leading up to the "holy day" – Epiphany, Pentecost, Veterans Day, St. Patrick's Day, Mother's and Father's Day, and/or other cultural holidays (Romans 14:5-9, Phillips). In late October, a Facebook post asked for ideas or teaching topics that would be appropriate for September. I (Milt) replied with the suggestion that Labor Day be emphasized. It would be an appropriate time for a topical lesson and discussion related to stewardship of God's creation, time, and money, the importance of work and discovering God's vocational calling, or the need to do all things well and for God's glory. The world, and media, in particular, fills children's minds with images and ideas that are often not biblical and rooted in a secular or materialistic worldview. During future labor days, will students remember it as a day for picnics and retail sales, or will they recall the biblical truths that were impressed upon them over time in your children's ministry? (Appendix C provides suggestions for additional celebration themes.)

Rather than ignoring a "secular" celebration, use the occasion to counter the world's thinking with an enduring biblical truth.

Mythic-literal Faith

Mythic-literal faith (stage two) can also be referred to as narrative faith (Fowler). It is during this time that faith stories are the primary focus. Children during the early concrete operations stage can now begin to think in more logical ways, form literal interpretations, and make connections between stories to form the framework for God's redemptive story. Throughout this stage, children accept instruction coming from those in authority as true, but their strong sense of justice and literal interpretations can shade these truths. For example, children during this stage may form the belief that if one does good, then good things will happen, but if one is bad, then something bad will follow.[9] It is, therefore, important that opportunities to emphasize God's grace be emphasized and that justice is taught along with compassion and mercy. No one sets out to develop a works-based faith, but when developmental immaturity is offered a diet of moral lessons, works-based faith can develop and often is the result.

Teachers must keep in mind that their way of thinking and understanding is not yet the way of the children within their classrooms. Children do not yet grasp the bigger picture (the whole) but instead focus on literal interpretations of the parts. The Apostle Paul worded it this way,

> "When I was a child, I spoke like a child, I thought like a child, I reasoned like a child. When I became a man, I gave up childish ways. For now, we see in a mirror dimly, but then face to face. Now I know in part, then I shall know fully..."
>
> 1 Corinthians 13:11-12 (NET)

The impressionistic experiences and celebrations of stage one serve as the foundation for telling the biblical narrative, God's story, during this stage. God again provides the curriculum through the presentation of His word in story format throughout the Old and New Testaments. It is the biblical narrative that, if learned during the elementary years, will serve as the foundation for the development of a Christ-centered worldview. George Barna, in his book on developing spiritual champions, writes:

> "By the age of nine, most of the moral and spiritual foundations of a child are in place...It seems that by the time he or she is nine, the child shifts mental gears and begins to use the cues he or she receives from that point forward to either confirm or challenge an existing perspective (*worldview*). It also appears that by the time the child has reached this age, it is much more difficult to change an existing view than to form a new view." [10]

Barna's research also found that most children's ministries touch upon 20 to 40 Bible stories each year, but these stories are often repeated year after year with little or no change or emphasis.[11] The consequence of this approach is students who by middle and high school believe they have heard it all and "know everything there is to know about the Christian faith." Churches often are satisfied that children can "identify the basic contours of the stories and can describe some details related to the key characters, but the young people are clueless regarding the fundamental principles and lessons to be drawn from those stories."[12]

In their book, *A Practical Guide to Culture: Helping the Next Generation Navigate Today's World,* John Stonestreet and Brett Kunkle identify another concern by referencing a statement made by Francis Schaeffer: "The basic problem of Christians is that they have seen [the world] in bits and pieces instead of totals."[13] They go on to apply Schaeffer's statement within our culture today:

> ...we could also say it's how many of us view the Scriptures: in bits and pieces, a disconnected collection of verses and stories designed to instruct us, depending on our predilections, in the way of morality, happiness, or financial prosperity...the Bible is more than a book of morality and religion. Fundamentally, it's a narrative. It tells the Story of the world, from the creation to the new creation.[14]

We can and must do better by attending to a vision that takes children beyond facts to application and beyond stories to God's one story, the story that "accurately describes reality, including what has gone wrong and how God will bring history to its conclusion according to His purposes."[15] In light of its importance, teaching God's one story will be examined more closely in chapter seven.

Synthetic-Conventional Faith

Knowing that children are on different developmental timelines, it is expected that some students may be moving into the next level of faith development as early as the fifth grade. Even though their thinking may not fully represent this stage, teachers should provide the scaffolding that enables students to reach a higher level. By the end of the previous stage, their faith story and beliefs have been learned. I (Milt) sometimes refer to this next level as "conforming faith" since the ideas of others (parents, teachers, and peers) are accepted, with little or no examination, as their own. Up to this point, others have been packing their bag of beliefs, and they, in order to conform, are content to carry this bag and its contents. After all, what preteen (ages 10 to 12) wants to be different?

Their developing ability to think more critically and seek autonomy pushes them to question what they have been carrying within their bag. Don't be surprised if one day they take a belief and question its validity. Don't panic, but if it should occur, welcome it, instead. They will increasingly become aware that not everyone believes what they do, and the media and pop culture are actively influencing their values and beliefs, as well. If students are going to choose their faith and make it their own, they will need to examine each belief and decide what they will place back into their bag. So, if questioning begins among your fifth graders, then listen intently and be ready to admit that you too once asked a similar question. Prepare yourself and be ready to answer questions like:

- How do we know that the Bible is true?
- Is Jesus the only way to Heaven?
- If God is good all the time, then why do bad things happen?
- How can God be one God and three persons at the same time?
- But what if the people never had an opportunity to hear the Gospel? Will they be saved?

In all cases, notice how their thinking has matured. Questions of this nature would not have occurred during previous stages due to their more limited ability to examine content from varying perspectives. This questioning is a sign that they are cognitively and spiritually maturing. Accept the questions as steps on the path to making faith their own! Begin your response with:

- That is a question that many people ask. I am glad you too want to think about this.
- Can you share with me why you are asking?
- Good question. This is how I have come to understand this, but you may want to talk this over with your parents, as well.

- I really want to help you answer this question. Here is what I believe, but perhaps you will also allow me to think about it a bit more and provide both of us with some additional answers or insights from other sources.
- That is a great question! I do not know the answer. Let's search the Bible and see what God says about it.

Do your homework and recall questions that you may have been asked in the past. Build your own age-appropriate apologetic, but don't force questioning. They will ask when they are ready. A quick online search of resources related to "tween" or middle school apologetics will help with this assignment.[16] I have personally found Robert Ferris's book, *Intimate & True: Bible truths in Simple Terms*, to also be a helpful resource. His granddaughter encouraged him to write this book during a homeschool doctrine course, and she felt his insights would also help other homeschoolers to understand theology.[17] Another good book is Brian Dollar's *Talk Now and Later*, where he helps parents learn to talk openly about hard topics with which their children might wrestle.

Extending Knowledge and Beliefs into Practice

- Create a classroom community that is not only safe physically but emotionally. Safe classrooms are developmentally appropriate and well-managed. They are free of putdowns and all bullying. When children know they are in a safe environment, then they feel more comfortable asking hard questions.
- Offer warm as opposed to cold interactions. Warm interactions offer expressions of love, thankfulness, care, and respect. Relationships are essential to transformational teaching.
- Provide bulletin boards or murals that visually depict principles drawn from the truths of Scripture—principles and truths that are the foundation for a biblical worldview and the children's daily lives.
- When preparing to teach, use a "backward design." Begin by asking yourself why you are teaching the lesson. What difference can it make in the lives of your students? How will this lesson or experience contribute to the accomplishment of the mission and vision of the elementary children's ministry?
- Study, learn, and practice telling God's big story. Start by reading Kevin DeYoung's *The Biggest Story* (also available in DVD format). [18]

- Share your own story (testimony) or time in which you entered into God's story.
- Display a redemptive story timeline and refer to it during teaching in order to weave biblical teaching into a single tapestry.
- Refer often to the opportunity that has been given to each student to enter into and become part of *the* story.
- Develop your holy day curriculum that is a unique expression of your church and its beliefs (i.e., observing a liturgical calendar). Establish these celebrations as a distinctive element of your children's ministry program.
- Have a "prayer box" in which students can place anonymous prayer requests.

Reflect and Respond

1. Think about your student's attitudes. Do behaviors reflect feelings of security, joy, confidence, and a desire to be in your children's ministry? What difference does it make?

2. What messages are the students receiving through your attitudes, verbal interactions, and body language?

3. In what ways do your classrooms reflect a Christian worldview? What might be done to better communicate truth through the classroom visuals?

4. Does your current curriculum honor the principle of one grand narrative? To what degree is it repetitive across the years? What changes might be needed?

5. Are celebrations used to communicate truth? How might the curriculum create additional opportunities to build faith-centered memories?

When integrated into one's life,
the truth becomes meaningful,
as opposed to abstract, and
this is an especially important
step toward faith development
and spiritual formation.

Chapter Two

A Living Curriculum

"Therefore, I urge you, brethren, by the mercies of God, to present your bodies a living, and holy, sacrifice acceptable to God, which is your spiritual service of worship. And do not be conformed to this world, but be transformed by the renewing of your mind, so that you may prove what the will of God is, that which is good and acceptable and perfect."
Romans 12:1-2

"However, you are not in the flesh but in the Spirit, if indeed the Spirit of God dwells in you. But if anyone does not have the Spirit of Christ, he does not belong to Him. If Christ is in you, though the body is dead because of sin, yet the spirit is alive because of righteousness."
Romans 8:8-11

"Be imitators of me (Paul), just as I also am of Christ."
1 Corinthians 11:1

"There can be no Christian education without a Christian teacher."
Frank Gaebelein[19]

A question that is often asked is, "What curriculum do you recommend?" Since the curriculum is the means to accomplish a program's desired outcomes, chapters three through six presented a faith-directed, Christ-centered worldview curriculum. The curriculum is life within a ministry community where teachers acknowledge God's presence and present worldview truths and character standards established by God and found in the Bible and where children are viewed as image-bearers who are uniquely and wonderfully made.

> This is a living curriculum, as opposed to a book or notebook that outlines weekly instruction.

This understanding of curriculum is especially important when considering the learning style or means through which children learn. As will become clear throughout the book, this curriculum is experience-based and under the moment-by-moment direction of a living, relational community: children, teachers, volunteers, and parents.

Biblically, parents are responsible for the faith formation of their children. The community of believers, or church, should stand ready to support parents whether through Sunday school, Vacation Bible School, parenting classes, nursery, or other ministry opportunities. Because some parents rely heavily on the church for help, it is crucial that children's ministry leaders and volunteers understand living curriculum. It is the parents and Bible teachers who have the mind of Christ and reflect a life in relationship with God. These important adults translate abstractions into experiences that are developmentally appropriate, understandable, and transferable into the life of the learner (Proverbs 27:27).

It is therefore impossible to conceive of children's ministry without teachers who have experienced rebirth and are committed to a life of learning, growing, following, and serving Christ. The life of the teacher demonstrates and validates the truths of the Bible (Matthew 7:20). Christian teachers, as they walk in the Spirit, fulfill the role of a prophet when they witness to and teach truth from God's perspective (1 John 1:1-3). They serve as priests, or mediators, as they bring the children's needs to God, and they serve as king through exercising their God-given authority as they guide and counsel students.[20]

The role and influence of the teacher bring a new level of understanding to James 3:1, where the reader is reminded that "…not many of you become teachers, my brethren, knowing that as such you will incur a stricter judgment." It is also important to apply the warning against causing "one of the little ones" to stumble. Children read their teachers long before they can read a book, and they continue to watch parents and teachers throughout childhood.

Within the third chapter of James, there is a warning directed to teachers regarding the impact of their behavior. Teachers through what they do and say model either the negative and positive impact of "bridling" behavior and "taming" the tongue (James 3:1-5). The content and tone of verbal interactions create an atmosphere of encouragement vs. discouragement, joy vs. anger, peace vs. fear, and warmth vs. coldness.

The Example of the Apostle Paul

The Apostle Paul understood the importance of modeling and accepted the responsibility. "Brethren, join in following my example and observe those who walk according to the pattern you have in us" (Philippians 3:17). He encouraged observation because he understood that what is seen is a powerful instructional tool. It is important to note that they were to follow not just his example but the Christians' pattern of living in relationship with one another.

Paul not only referenced himself as "living curriculum" but also parents and grandparents as they live their lives before their children. Paul's letters to Timothy acknowledge Timothy's sincere faith as being rooted in the faith of his grandmother Lois and his mother Eunice (1 Timothy 1:5 and 2 Timothy 3:14-15). The letters to Timothy were written to "encourage older believers to pass on their knowledge of Scripture to those who are younger in the faith," and "Paul charged Timothy to live a life beyond reproach, giving believers a standard to emulate."[21]

Because of modeling's instructional impact, Paul wept over the fact that *many* were walking in or demonstrating error as opposed to the truth because their god was their appetite and their minds were set on earthly things as opposed to heavenly citizenship (v. 18-20).

As one reads the epistles, or letters, that Paul sent to his students, one gains insight into the profile of an incarnational teacher.

Ministry Leaders, Teachers, and Volunteers (Models) Should:

- *"...walk in a manner worthy of the calling with which you have been called" (Ephesians 4:1).*
- *Have renewed minds that are characterized by humility and sound judgment (Romans 12:3, 16).*
- *Exercise their gifts (Romans 12:7-8).*
- *Love without hypocrisy, demonstrate empathy, and be devoted to and honor one another (Romans 12:10).*
- *Evidence diligence and perseverance during hard times (Romans 12:11-12).*
- *Show empathy and practice hospitality by inviting students into fellowship (Romans 12:13, 15).*
- *Respect what is right and never repay evil with evil (Romans 12:17).*
- *Be perceived as gentle, patient, tolerant (Ephesians 4:2).*
- *Put aside anger and abusive speech (Colossians 3:8).*
- *Show compassion and kindness (Colossians 3:12).*
- *Allow the peace and Word of Christ to dwell and rule in their hearts (Colossians 3:15-16).*

The Importance of Community

Spiritual formation happens within the context of community; therefore, life within the ministry classroom is another element of the living curriculum. Classroom climate may be a second factor, but it too is controlled by a teacher's temperament, behavior, and instructional practices.

There will be times, on the occasional down day, when the classroom climate may feel a bit chilly, but when an uncomfortable coldness becomes the normal temperature, the climate may negate the message of the Gospel. Ministry leaders, in their role as shepherds of their staff, must be responsible for reading and controlling the climate through monitoring the teachers' well-being, providing encouragement, listening, and, when needed, pointing out a blind spot or unacceptable behavior (harshness, impatience, put-downs, sarcasm, etc.).

The Epistles reveal Paul's interactions with his students and provide insight into Paul's other-directed values and relationships. Paul referred to Silvanus, Timothy, and himself as being gentle among the Thessalonians and compared their care to that of "a nursing mother tenderly caring for her own children." He also referred to their having a "fond affection" and finding pleasure in not only imparting the Gospel of God but their own lives on their behalf. Paul and his team also had hearts of a father in that they exhorted, encouraged, and implored each of them as a father would his children (1 Thessalonians 2:7-11).

Paul prayed for and encouraged his "classroom" of new believers. He told them that he thanked God for them and that he longed to see them and assured them that he always remembered them in his prayers (Philippians 1:3-8). His prayers for them were joyful because they participated in the Gospel together, and he envisioned God perfecting them in Christ and enabling them to abound in love and be filled with the fruit of righteousness (Philippians 1:9-11).

One can easily imagine the impact on students when being told by Paul that they were his hope, joy, glory, and crown of exultation (1 Thessalonians 2:19-20).

Transformational ministries are places where:

- The Holy Spirit empowers teachers to reflect the fruit of the Spirit.
- Children are unconditionally loved and accepted.
- Relationships are warm as opposed to cold or merely task-oriented.
- Children experience developmentally appropriate instruction and where varying levels of readiness are accommodated.
- Trust abounds, and children feel safe.
- All children think that they belong through opportunities to use their gifts and experience success.
- Children regularly laugh, play, work, and share with one another.
- Children are well-managed, and biblical principles of discipline are exercised.
- Relationships are infused with grace.
- Students are introduced to *shalom*---the way things, in Christ, can and should be.

The Ongoing Battle

Ministry to the next generation, whether early childhood, elementary, or adolescent, is on a mission to lay the foundational elements of a Christian worldview and, most importantly, for a life in Christ. In light of the weightiness of this responsibility, you may find yourself saying, "I can't. I am not able!" This, however, is an important confession in that it is at this point where Jesus says, "But I can!"

> The Christian life and the life of an incarnational teacher reflect dependence upon the Spirit of God and the body of Christ, not one's independence.

John Ortberg, in *Everybody's Normal till You Get to Know Them*, discusses an obstacle to creating community. Even though we were created for relationships, our flesh makes maintaining community difficult.[22] Ortberg writes,

> When you deal with human beings, you have come to the "as is" corner of the universe. …One of the great marks of maturity is to accept the fact that everybody comes "as is." …Of course, the most painful part of this is realizing that I am in the "as is" department, as well.
>
> Every one of us pretends to be healthier and kinder than we really are; we all engage in what might be called "depravity management." … Every one of us—all we like sheep—has habits we can't control, past deeds we can't undo, flaws we can't correct. This is the cast of characters God has to work with (14-17).

"All we like sheep" describes all the members of the ministry team—directors, teachers, parents, and the children. If community is to be created and life in Christ modeled, then it must begin with admitting that one cannot do this on one's own. Everyone within a children's ministry program must acknowledge and deal with the "as is" flaw. Paul, once again, serves as a model.

He openly acknowledged that he struggled with his weaknesses.

He too struggled with sin and inconsistency.

He too was flawed. He speaks of this in Romans 7 when he writes,

> *"For we know that the law is spiritual—but I am unspiritual, sold into slavery to sin. For I don't understand what I am doing. For I do not do what I want—instead, I do what I hate. But if I do what I don't want, I agree that the law is good. But now it is no longer me doing it, but sin that lives in me. For I know that nothing good lives in me, that is, in my flesh. For I want to do the good, but I cannot do it. For I do not do the good I want, but I do the very evil I do not want! Now if I do what I do not want, it is no longer me doing it but sin that lives in me.*
>
> *So, I find the law that when I want to do good, evil is present with me. For I delight in the law of God in my inner being. But I see a different law in my members waging war against the law of my mind and making me captive to the law of sin that is in my members. Wretched man that I am! Who will rescue me from this body of death?"*
>
> *Romans 7:14-24 (ESV)*

Paul also testified to the solution.

He chose to live under the power of the Holy Spirit because he accepted the fact that in the flesh he couldn't, but in the Spirit, he could:

> *"For those who live according to the flesh have their outlook shaped by the things of the flesh, but those who live according to the Spirit have their outlook shaped by the things of the Spirit. For the outlook of the flesh is death, but the outlook of the Spirit is life and peace because the outlook of the flesh is hostile to God, for it does not submit to the law of God, nor is it able to do so. Those who are in the flesh cannot please God."*
>
> ***"You, however, are not in the flesh but in the Spirit,** if indeed the Spirit of God lives in you. Now if anyone does not have the Spirit of Christ, this person does not belong to him. But if Christ is in you, your body is dead because of sin, but the Spirit is your life because of righteousness. Moreover, if the Spirit of the one who raised Jesus from*

the dead lives in you, the one who raised Christ from the dead will also make your mortal bodies alive through His Spirit who lives in you."

Romans 8:5-1 (ESV)

You have heard it said that those who do not acknowledge warfare will lose the battle.

> The enemy of our faith is not on the sideline rooting for our success within our children's ministry.

The devil will actively work to draw attention away from the truth, tempt teachers and children to yield to the desires of the flesh, lie to us about who we are and our worth as individuals, and bring about divisions within our programs.

We must, therefore, hear Paul's exhortation to "put on the full armor of God so that you will be able to stand firm against the schemes of the devil" (Ephesians 6:11). Paul goes on to say that "with all prayer and petition pray at all times in the Spirit" (v.19). He prayed for perseverance and boldness and that he might speak as he ought in making known the Gospel (v. 20).

Paul acted upon the truth and not his feelings.

He acknowledged the fact that he couldn't and as a result became dependent on the Spirit and prayer. He knew that those he discipled, in their own strength, would likewise be unable, and so he prayed that his students would be "rooted and established in the love of Christ and that the Spirit would strengthen and empower them" (Ephesians 3:14-18, ESV).

> Transformational teachers accept the responsibility to die to self and become more and more like Christ.

Dr. Robertson McQuilken, former president of Columbia International University, shared a straightforward formula for realizing a victorious life. The first step is the acknowledgment and confession of specific sins. Confession must then be followed by "targeted" prayer and petition for the strength needed to stand firm and not give in to temptation. During this warfare, one should focus on meditating and memorizing related truths from God's Word, and finally, invite another staff person or ministry volunteer to join them in warfare, share in their struggle, and hold them accountable.[23]

Extending Knowledge and Beliefs into Practice

- Regularly study and encourage one another in the spiritual disciplines related to dependence on Christ and "walking in the spirit."
- Pray for and embrace the fruit of the Spirit.
- Practice child-directed as opposed to curriculum-directed instruction. Know the children across all strands of their development and align practices with readiness as a means of limiting stress and experiencing success. View children as individuals.
- Demonstrate enthusiasm throughout your interactions.
- Voice love and concern for your students.
- Pray for each child and their family.
- Claim your ministry area through a prayer walk around the room(s) for Christ and His work each week.

Reflect and Respond

1. Stand back and frame the climate within your classroom or the classrooms within your program. Identify the climate that characterizes your ministry community and its gathering places. Is the community warm or cold in nature? What steps can be taken to represent *shalom* better?

2. Compare your dispositions to those of an incarnational teacher. Are you able to invite your children to imitate you? Journal your conclusion.

3. Identify and confess areas of personal weakness or inconsistency. Are you willing to change and walk in a new direction? If so, what steps will you take?

4. When you fall short – and at times, you will – what is your response to the children? Can you recall times when you confessed behaviors that were out of alignment with Christ and, therefore, not a reflection of Christ in your classroom?

5. Have you expanded your community to include the parents? What characterizes your relationship with parents? How often do you talk to them? What is the nature of your communication? Do you welcome them or try to avoid them?

6. The next time someone asks you what curriculum you use, what will be your answer?

Final Note: As you are walked through the process of laying the foundation for a Christian worldview, you will no doubt sense the similarity of means within many of the chapters. This is because the means can and should be integrated. Just as a worldview is an integrated whole, so too are the means for developing a child's faith. The means are not independent instructional elements, but rather, when integrated, the whole of the students' experiences.

Chapter Three

Worldview Integration: Reality

All things were created through Him and for Him. And He is before all things, and in Him, all things consist.

Colossians 1:16-17

For the LORD is good and His love endures forever; His faithfulness continues through all generations.

Psalm 100:5 (NIV)

For the things that are seen are temporary, but the things that are not seen are eternal.

II Corinthians. 4:18

Even though teaching from the perspective of a biblical or Christian worldview is an often-used phrase within Christian educational settings, an understanding of the elements of a worldview is often lacking. Ministry experiences, through their environment, curriculum, and values, do communicate a worldview. The world, however, also teaches. Through daily exposure, children are learning and forming their worldview via the attitudes, beliefs, and behaviors of their family, peers, social media platforms, and the media at-large. Without an intentional focus on a distinctively different biblical worldview in the home, church, and, when possible, a Christian school, children will develop a "mixed bag" of answers to life's important questions.

Branson S. Howse defines worldview as,

> "...the lens, glasses, framework, or grid through which you look at the world and every issue of life...your worldview is the foundation of your ideas and values and your ideas and values are the foundation of your conduct."[24]

Even though worldview deals with philosophy, and the vocabulary and concepts often require higher-level thinking, children can develop basic understandings during the elementary years. As previously noted, a child's moral foundation, according to Barna, is in place by age 9, and worldview is developed between the ages of 18 months and age 13.[25] So, ministry and programs should be intentional about making worldview a more explicit part of instruction.

This chapter and the three that follow will examine the major worldview questions.

- What is the nature of reality and the universe?
- What is the source of knowledge, and how does one know it is true?
- What is of value, right and wrong, and what determines it?
- What defines us as humans? What are our nature and purpose?

According to Stonestreet and Kunkle, how we answer any one of these questions will shape how we answer the others. For example, if there is no God who created the world (origin), then humans are just products of natural forces like any other life forms (identity). Or if Columbine High School shooters Dylan Klebold and Eric Harris were correct in their belief that there is no life after death (destiny), then they faced no eternal consequences for their actions (morality)...our fundamental beliefs about life matter.[26]

The Concept of God

The key to any philosophy of life is one's concept of God: who He is, what He has done, and what His relationship is to the world and the people He created. Mark Fakkema writes that "Christian philosophy is the romance of seeing all things as one whole with God as the ultimate."[27] A worldview has a focal point, and in the case of a Christian worldview, the focal point is transcendent or other-worldly. Fakkema's reference to "ultimate" implies that God is the reference or focal point for all things. God is the reason or purpose of everything else. The Apostle Paul wrote of this truth in his letter to the Romans: "For from Him and through Him and to Him are all things" (Romans 11:36a).

To the Corinthians, he emphasized the centrality of Jesus Christ as the foundation upon which he built his life but also upon which others must build theirs:

> **"For no man can lay a foundation other than the one which is laid, which is Jesus Christ"**
>
> 1 Corinthians 3:11

So too, the church's ministry to children will start with God and reveal Him through His creation, Scripture, and in the person of Jesus Christ and the work of the Holy Spirit.

In Psalm 78, we are commanded to tell the next generation the "...praises of the Lord, and His strength and His wondrous works that He has done" (v. 4). Therefore, within our ministries, we must "diligently teach" (Deut. 6:7) the Bible and introduce them to Jesus, the Word made flesh, who is the Way, the truth, and the Life. We not only teach, but we pray that the Holy Spirit will empower us, so that we can know and model truth and that the children will be drawn to their Savior and live a life filled with hope and purpose.

We must not limit the stories of God to the works done in and among the people of Israel and the early church, but like them, we should tell of the works He has done for us, as well. Our personal stories, the stories of His daily presence and answered prayers, bring His presence into our ministries. Many Bible curricula leave out the part about living God's Word on a daily basis (or life application). However, children at this age begin to explore the "whys" of life, which means Bible teachers need to be prepared to explain why their students need to know God, Jesus, and the Holy Spirit.

If God is to become the answer to the questions regarding the nature of reality, then we have to speak and demonstrate the reality of God in our own lives. As teachers show regard for Him, praise Him, and lead the class in talking to Him, the foundation for "putting their confidence in Him and not *forgetting* the works of God" (Psalm 78:7) is laid.

When teaching worldview, it is important that we keep a child's language development and ways of thinking (cognitive development) in mind. This should not be reason to shy away from philosophy and theology, but it is reason to identify truths that can be made meaningful through experience (past and present) and age-appropriate language.

Chapters three through six overview and answer each of the primary worldview questions. During instruction, children will also add their own questions, and the answers to their questions will not only contribute to their understanding but give you insight into their thinking and understanding. A Christian's worldview beliefs and values are learned not only from knowing what the beliefs are but how Christian beliefs (theism) differ from other worldviews. As the differences are recognized or understood, the process of equipping students to recognize oppositional worldviews (naturalism, humanism, and pantheism) will likewise be developed.

The Questions Regarding Reality:

Is there a god? Is there only one god, or are there many gods?

God is in Heaven, while at the same time, we are always in His presence because all things at all times are in His presence (omnipresence). God has given a book, called the Bible, about Himself and what He has done and is doing. As we hear His story and words, we will get to know Him better. In the Bible, God is referred to as our Father, the Lord, King of Kings, and Savior. He is the one and only true God—He alone has always been (eternal). Everything else has a beginning and an end. This is why God said His name is "I AM."[28] "God is one God, and God is three persons in an everlasting relationship with one another..."[29]

God hears us and wants us to talk to Him through prayer.

> When we pray, we can talk with Him like we talk to our parents and friends in the classroom.

Because He is God, we will worship Him by obeying, offering praise through singing, and serving Him.

What is God like? Where is He?

Because God is God, there are many things that we may not understand, but God has told us about Himself in the Bible, and He sent His son Jesus to live on Earth so that we could understand more about what He is like. He also sent the Holy Spirit to teach us about God. Jesus and the Holy Spirit are God. Some things, like God being three persons (Father, Son, and Holy Spirit), are a mystery.

> But since God is God, it should not surprise us that some things about Him are difficult to understand.

The Bible tells us that God knows everything; that He is good all the time; that He cares for (does good things) and watches over us; that He loves us and wants us to know Him and be friends with His son, Jesus. God is not pleased when we disobey Him or do things that are wrong. He wants us to tell Him what we did, tell Him we are sorry, and ask His forgiveness.

Even though God is present in all places, His throne is in Heaven. Heaven is a real place where people who know God and allow Jesus to be the boss of their life will someday go to live with Him. The Bible describes Heaven as a beautiful, peaceful place where there is no more sadness.

Sometimes, people talk to or worship gods made of wood and stone. These made-up gods are called "idols." Anything that we think is more important than God, like sports, money, toys, and computers, can also be an idol.

How did this world come into being?

God made the world and all that lives in it by speaking. He said, "Let there be" and it was. In this way, He made the sun, moon, stars, the Earth, oceans, plants, animals, and you and me. He is all-powerful (omnipotence), and this is why we call Him the Creator. Only God can create from nothing. When we create, we use things that already exist. God designed everything to fit and work perfectly together because He is also all-knowing. His creation shows us that God is really amazing, and He and His words are powerful.

Are the things I can touch and see the only things that are real?

There are things that we have never seen or touched that are real. This includes an unseen world that is as real as the world we live in. There are many things that are so far away in space that we cannot see them, but they are surely there. Heaven is an example. God's book, the Bible, tells us that this is true:

> …We know that Heaven is God's home (Deuteronomy 26:15 and 2 Chronicles 30:27). It is where He lives (Matthew 6:9, 16:17). We also know that Heaven will be populated by God's people (Revelation 7:9-10), that God's will is done there (Matthew 6:10), that is a place of joy (Psalm 16:11) and righteousness (2 Peter 3:13), and that it is free from sorrow, death, and pain (Revelation 21:4).[30]

Angels are also part of the unseen world. The Bible says that there are millions of angels who serve as messengers from God and are part of the way God is involved in our world and lives. They guide, guard, protect and help God's people. Angels are created beings like people, but when people die, they do not become angels.

Other Worldviews: Reality

The Question	Naturalism	Humanism	Pantheism[31]
What is real?	What can be seen, touched, and verified by science	This world is all there is. Only matter is real. Man is matter and the central focus and being.	Reality is not distinguishable.
Belief regarding God	Nature (the laws of nature) Impersonal	No belief in God, so man is responsible for solving the world's problems.	God is an impersonal force. God is in all things.

Open the Window of Opportunity

From a developmental perspective, children prior to this stage of development are by nature open to God as a reality. Zuck and Clark invoke Piaget's reference to a child's creative, imaginative thinking and magical explanations.[32] Childhood's way of thinking, likewise, opens a window of opportunity for belief in God as well as the idea that if God is God, then He could at the same time be one God and three persons. However, by fourth grade, evidence and rationality will begin to influence a child's faith. Students will ask questions to clarify ideas that used to be accepted on the authority of the teacher. Students now look to the teacher and parents to explain what they have trouble comprehending or accepting. Prior to delving into an answer that is beyond the reason for inquiry or remains above their level of conceptualization, you might respond first with, "What is your thinking, or what made you think of this question?" Then answer their concern as simply as possible. End your explanation with, "Does that help?"

A child's need for safety is critical to their social development, and unless a student feels safe, their spiritual development may be negatively impacted. Create an environment where it is safe to question. Positive experiences with inquiry will set the stage for asking the questions that make beliefs their own. This is exemplified in the adult world, as well. In recent years there are numerous examples of well-known Christians who after serving in ministry began to question and gradually "deconstruct" their faith. The testimonies of these individuals often include reference to an unquestioned acceptance of their church's evangelical beliefs. From the perspective of faith development "deconstructing" may be rooted in a lack of opportunity to question and work through and uncover answers within the safety of the church's classrooms.

Our children need a safe atmosphere with caring church leaders who will allow them to wrestle with God's truth. Do not be afraid of the questions. Pray for the children God has placed under your care. Teach them the foundation so that when they do question, they know that God is the one who is always faithful.

Extending Knowledge and Beliefs into Practice

1. Provide a permanent bulletin board centered upon God as Creator. Use the bulletin board to portray the days of creation and the design, patterns, creativity, and beauty found in creation.

2. Use story as a primary instructional strategy. Include:
   a. Stories about God's power over creation and Jesus' miracles
   b. Stories that illustrate what God is like
   c. Stories about what God has done and is doing in your personal life

3. Speak with God through prayer. Incorporate regular as well as spontaneous times of prayer. Be sure to model statements of praise and gratitude. Make notes regarding prayer requests and be sure to refer to God and His love and care as prayers are answered

4. Practice joyful and active times of worship. Design worship for this age group as opposed to bringing the children to gatherings where middle school students (due to intimidation factors) are also present. Limit "large group" experiences to holiday celebrations and other special occasions. JumpStart3 and Yancy create wonderful Scripture memory and worship songs.

5. Create and maintain disciplined, safe, learning environments. There should be several important classroom rules that can lovingly and consistently be addressed. Establish classrooms as a "no put-down or bullying zone." Teach the children why the rules are important and explain the consequences not only for the child but others when rules are not followed. In so doing, children learn to obey parents and teachers as the starting point for obeying God.

6. Use children's literature and other resources to supplement or complement your Bible lessons:
   a. Groth, Jeanette. 1986. *Prayer: Learning How to Talk to God.* St. Louis: Concordia.
   b. Marxhausen, Joanne. *Heaven Is a Wonderful Place.* St. Louis: Concordia. This is also useful in learning about the nature of man.
   c. Lewis, C.S. 1995. *Chronicles of Narnia.* New York: Scholastic.
   d. Sproul, R.C. 2008. *The Prince's Poison Cup.* Florida: Reformation Trust Publishing.
   e. Arch book series. 1982. St. Louis: Concordia.
   f. Travis, Melissa Cain. 2013. *How Do We Know God Is Really There?* Indiana: Apologia Press

g. Giglio, Louie. 2017. *Indescribable: 100 Devotions for Kids About God and Science.* Thomas Nelson

h. Giglio, Louie, 2019. *How Great is Our God: 100 Indescribable Devotions for Kids About God and Science.* Thomas Nelson

i. Bergren, Lisa T. 2008. *God Gave Us Heaven.* Colorado Spring: Waterbrook Press.

j. Tomlin, Chris. 2016 *Good, Good Father.* Nashville: Tommy Nelson.

7. Memorize Scripture that answers the worldview question dealing with reality. See Appendix E for a worldview memory verse curriculum.

8. Integrate children's worship songs into lessons and times of worship. This list includes many well-known standards. The lyrics and videos are easily accessed through YouTube and online searches. Songs with movement add impact and facilitate the child's memory of the lyrics. Add your own favorites based upon whether or not the lyrics answer questions related to reality.

a. "What a Mighty God We Serve"

b. "God Is Good All the Time"

c. "God of Creation" (Mary Rice Hopkins)

d. "How Great Is Our God?"

e. "The Lord Is My Rock"

f. "Our God Is an Awesome God"

g. "The Trinity Song" (Folker)

h. "My God Is So Big"

i. "My Father's House"

j. "God Is So Wonderful" (Parker Stephens)

k. "I Want to Praise You for My Voice" (Character)

l. "My God Is So Big and So Strong and So Mighty"

m. "I Have a Friend Who Really Loves Me"

n. "God Is Always with Us" (Group Publishing)

o. "God Forgave" (Group Publishing)

p. "God Is Listening" (Group Publishing)

q. "I Sing the Mighty Power of God" (Group Publishing)

r. "One True God" (Group Publishing)

s. "My God Is Powerful" (Group Publishing)

t. "When We Pray" (Yancy)

u. "I Can Count on God" (Yancy)

v. "God Does Great Things" (Yancy)

w. "1 Samuel 16:7 (The Lord Looks at the Heart)" (JumpStart3)

x. "My Lord, What a Morning" (African spiritual)

y. "Bless the Lord, Oh My Soul" (African spiritual)

z. "When God First Brought Us Back" (African spiritual"

9. Learn the words to classic hymns as a means of connecting with and preserving the past and internalizing a Christian worldview (theological truths). Listen to a variety of styles (traditional, Gospel, contemporary, etc.). In lieu of singing, consider choral reading as an alternative.

a. "Great Is Thy Faithfulness"

b. "Praise to the Lord, the Almighty"

c. "Holy, Holy, Holy"

d. "A Mighty Fortress Is Our God"

e. "Take It to the Lord in Prayer"

f. "Oh God, Our Help in Ages Past"

g. "Standing on the Promises"

h. "When I Survey the Wondrous Cross"

i. "We Gather Together"

j. "Joyful, Joyful, We Adore Thee"

k. "Come, Thou Almighty King"

l. "How Great Thou Art"

m. "Immortal, Invisible, God Only Wise"

n. "I Sing the Almighty Power of God"

o. "This Is My Father's World"

p. "All Creatures of Our God and King"

q. "His Eye Is on the Sparrow"

10. In addition to the worldview comparison table found on page 38 and also within chapters 4-6, you may want to refer to *Worldviews: A Children's Introduction to Missions*. This book, written by Sarah Lewis and published by Pioneers, teaches the worldviews of the major unreached people groups and is an excellent way to integrate worldviews when teaching missions.[33]

Education must be centered in reality: God-centered/Christ-centered. To leave God (Christ) out is to misunderstand reality and life and purpose. Teachers must have this worldview if he or she is to teach from it. The chief GOAL of education is that the student might know and love God.[34]

Reflect and Respond

1. Step back and "frame," or take a look, at the children's ministry areas. In what ways does the environment reflect God? Now, consider the area with children present. Apart from direct instruction, in what ways do ministry interactions reflect the presence of God?

2. Evaluate the Bible curriculum in light of the question of reality. Is worldview truth being taught? If so, provide specific examples. Is there a need to supplement the current curriculum?

3. Reflect upon your personal "God stories." What stories have you shared with the children? Identify additional stories. Think about a personal God story that aligns with a Bible story being taught. Examples: A story about personal healing, when God led or showed the way to go, when He gave strength and motivation to do something difficult, when obedience brought joy, when a hard time was a blessing, etc.

4. Examine the nature of your children's ministry worship time. Are these times of joy, movement, and engagement on the part of children? What can be done to better practice the presence of God and demonstrate praise and thanksgiving to Him?

5. In what ways are you assessing whether children are developing an understanding of the nature of reality? What are they able to tell you about God at the end of their time in your elementary ministry program? Means include interviewing, asking parents during a conversation what their children are saying about God, keeping a journal of comments children make in class, etc.

Chapter Four

Worldview Integration: Knowledge and truth

Sanctify them through Thy truth; Thy word is truth.

John 17:17

All Scripture is breathed out by God and profitable for teaching, for reproof, for correction, and for training in righteousness.

2 Timothy 3:16

Jesus said, "I am the way, the truth, and the life."

John 14:6 (ESV)

- What is truth?
- What can we know?
- How can we know?

"These questions must be raised by any philosopher. This may be the most important problem in philosophy. Unless it is possible to possess knowledge and to know the truth, it would be impossible to construct, let alone be sure of, any system of thought." [35] H. Gene Garrick

The nature of truth is a big issue today. The reigning epistemology (i.e., the theory of truth) in universities, the major media, and popular culture is constructivism. Constructivism begins from the observation that we all start from our own experience. As we attempt to make sense of our experience (with the help of our culture and our social networks, including our families), we "construct" opinions about what is real, what is good, and how things and events are related. We weave these into a perspective that we use to interpret life experiences and that we *assume to be the truth.*[36]

In light of the evasiveness of constructivism within our culture and educational philosophy as a whole, it is critical that the biblical viewpoint regarding truth be emphasized within the upper elementary grades. The truth about truth and how it can be known must be explicitly taught. If the next generation is to build a life upon more than man's ever-changing opinions, then declaring truth, based upon reality and not culture's man-centered ideas, must be the responsibility of the body of Christ and, thus, a critical objective of youth ministries.

> There are three options when answering the questions regarding the source of truth—nature, man, or a transcendent revelation (God).

Having established the Lord God as the ultimate reality and one in whom we can trust, it follows that whatever He would say would be true. Speaking falsely would disqualify God of His worthiness to take His place on the throne of Heaven and Earth. Our holy God has spoken and recorded His desires, commands, and redemptive plan in a book—the Bible. Arthur Holmes offered these reasonable assumptions:

"God reveals Himself to men created in His image…This revelation is general—in creation; it is personal—in Jesus Christ; it is written and propositional—in the Bible…All truth then is God's truth."[37] Since God reveals truth through nature or creation (general revelation), it can be said that God authored two books—the book of creation and the Bible." Additionally, He revealed, through the incarnation, the truth in the person of Jesus Christ, His Son (John 1:14).

Responding to Questions Regarding Truth:

Can we know what truth is?

The truth can be known by reading God's Word and in Jesus, "the word made flesh." Truth can also be found in creation. The "laws of nature" were also spoken by God when He said, "let there be." They are uncovered through scientific investigation and referred to as creation ordinances. The truths found in nature, in God's Word, and in Jesus are absolute because their source is reality—what is.

Is there one truth, or are there many different truths?

God has told us the truth, and Jesus did what was true because "He is the truth…" (John 14:6). There can only be one truth. Something cannot be true if contrary ideas, those different from God's, were also true. If, for example, God says that He alone is God, and someone else says there are many gods, then one of the statements must be false. God's Word has been written down, and since God said it and it is not in God's nature to lie, it will always remain true no matter what.

What are the sources of truth?

Truth is transcendent, given by God, as opposed to coming from man's thought or opinion. In addition to what God has told us in the Bible and what we see in the world He has made, Jesus, God's Son, is the truth. The Bible says that "all the treasures of wisdom and knowledge are hidden in Christ" (Colossians. 2:3) and that grace and truth came through Jesus Christ (John 1:17). Therefore, Jesus's words and teachings were true (John 8:45-46); His actions or behaviors were true (John 5:17); and His character (John 7:18) and relationships were true.[38]

God also has given us the Holy Spirit to guide us to the truth. The Spirit teaches us and helps us to understand and remember what is true and what is not true (John 14:26). It is the Holy Spirit that guided the people when they first wrote God's Word. The Spirit gave them God's thoughts and truths so that we, too, can know them. Both Jesus and the Holy Spirit are one with God, and thus all truth has been revealed to us in and through the Trinity.

The creation and how it works (creation laws) can be known through careful observation and when we study science. For example, when water is 32 degrees Fahrenheit or lower, it turns into ice. When water becomes really hot, it turns to steam, it evaporates, and this water, when it gets cool again, turns back to water and returns to the Earth as rain. When something is dropped, because of gravity, it falls. The laws of nature are true and keep the world working in a perfect and orderly way. When God *spoke* the world into being, God said that it was good. Natural laws, as revealed through scientific investigation (natural revelation), are both true and good.

Other Worldviews: Truth

The Question	Naturalism	Humanism	Pantheism
What is truth?	The only source of truth is scientific exploration or method. It is limited to the natural world or what can be discovered through the senses.	Truth stems from man's rationality. Truth is based upon individual and collective experiences and beliefs. It is relative to a person or situation. It is, therefore, subjective.	Truth is beyond grasp. It is found within the cosmos but cannot be grasped. It is found in everything because everything is spiritual.

God's Special Book

Because the Bible is a book authored by God, through the inspiration of the Holy Spirit, it should be viewed within the classroom as a special book. Children will develop this disposition through the modeling of the teacher. The Bible should have a special place within the classroom and be handled with the respect and care that is becoming of the truth. When teaching, I (Anne Marie) have the Bible open to the Scripture verses I am teaching. I will have the Bible either in my hands or right beside me because I want the children to understand that the story or principle I am teaching does not come from me but from God's Word. This is an easy way to help show the authority of Scripture.

If God is talking, then children should be encouraged to listen carefully because everything He says is important. Children should be taught that reading the Bible and memorizing its words are another way (in addition to prayer and worship) to spend time with God and show their love for Him.

The Bible should also be viewed as a special or unique book because God desires that the truth be not only read and learned but also acted upon or obeyed. Therefore, a Bible study should end with the question, "What is God asking me to do?"

> Too often, the sole objective for a Bible story or lesson is a desire for the children to retell the story or restate a command like, "honor your mother and father."

Using the example of honoring and obeying, we might base our lesson on the story of Jonah. After telling or reviewing the story, talk about the definition of obedience and honor. Did Jonah obey and honor God? Can you defend your answer? What would obedience have looked like for Jonah? Then, transition to the children you are teaching. Focus on what a boy or girl who demonstrates obedience and honor would do or not do.

This is important if the child is to develop the habit of responding to the truth. A heartfelt desire to obey on the part of children must be accompanied by understanding what God desires and then imagining or planning ways to respond. The children should likewise be led in a discussion of the ways in which they can honor and obey their parents. Their responses might include ideas like do what they say without fussing (like Jonah did), thank them for their care, speak in a loving way, and offer to help them.

If helping them is a suggestion, then that should be followed up with the ways in which they might help, including roleplaying a situation where help might be welcomed by the parent. They should also be led to consider what *not* honoring would look like. Showing what does not fit a concept (or character trait) is an important aspect of concept formation.

When integrated into one's life, the truth becomes meaningful, as opposed to abstract, and this is an especially important step toward faith development and spiritual formation.

The Creation "Book"

God's creation "book" should also be viewed with awe. God has revealed Himself through this "book," as well (Romans 1:20-24). The creation ordinances (laws of nature) should be studied through observation and then a connection to God's love and provision through the realization of the orderliness or design of creation.

Children's ministry can include simple classroom science experiments, object lessons, and nature walks. Field trips to a local park or children's interactive museum provide opportunities to point out God's "intelligent design." Children should be led to respond to His wisdom through praise and worship and through obeying God's command to care for creation. Show them how to care for their immediate environment by providing opportunities to participate in the stewardship of God's creation.

> Through these means, truth is impacting the child rationally, emotionally, and actively through individual involvement.

The overarching goal is that children see truth as originating in, and revealed by, God in creation and the Bible so that the foundation for the declaration that "All truth is God's truth" becomes a part of the child's understanding and emerging worldview.

Discerning truth

> For though we live as human beings, we do not wage war according to human standards, for the weapons of our warfare are not human weapons but are made powerful by God for tearing down strongholds. We tear down arguments and every arrogant obstacle that is raised up against the knowledge of God, and we take every thought captive to make it obey Christ.
>
> 2 Corinthians 10:3-5 (NET)

Our students have lived their lives in the midst of an ongoing culture war. It is warfare centered upon opposing ideas. Unless our children are taught that there is a tug-of-war between opposing worldviews, they will be taken captive or swept into the world's thinking. We are surrounded with opposing truth claims—God's thought vs. the thoughts of men. The presence of fake news is not the only threat; there is a threat brought on by arguments that oppose God's truth.

Elementary children are old enough to begin recognizing that not everything held up as truth is true, that not everything considered moral is moral, and that it is not OK to engage in *whatever* is desired or needed to be happy. Critical thinking or discernment based on Scripture is the weapon, and it must be developed. Our vision for children reaches beyond their knowing the Word to standing on the Word.

> "Christians and their children need to be able to decide what to believe, to distinguish between what is true and what is false. God anticipated this when dealing with the people of Israel. In their context, the question was how to recognize a true prophet, a prophet who could be trusted to speak God's messages faithfully. God provides two complimentary answers to that question in the book of Deuteronomy."[39]

- **The rational test**: If what is being said or claimed does not align or agree with what God has said, then it should not be accepted as truth.
- **The empirical test**: If what is being said or claimed is not consistent with what is known to be true from the observation within the physical world or the creation ordinances, then it should not be accepted as truth. Something true is always consistent with what has been shown through investigated evidence.

> "Dear friends, do not believe every spirit but test the spirits to determine if they are from God because many false prophets have gone out into the world."
>
> 1 John 4:1 (NET)

God's two books, therefore, provide the benchmark against which the validity of ideas must be measured. Critical thinking always involves a judgment. Worldview detectives are critical thinkers who gather and compare evidence.

- Is what I am reading true?
- Does this agree with what God has said in the Bible?
- Are these ideas acceptable? Are they moral?

- Should I apply or reject this idea?
- Does this represent the actions and thoughts that represent a biblical worldview?

In the summer of 2019, I (Milton) attended the Lowrie Center for Christian School Education's Distinctive Teaching and Learning Conference hosted on the campus of Lexington Christian Academy. At that conference, I was introduced to Elizabeth Urbanowicz, an apologist who focuses on teaching worldview to children during their elementary years. Her organization, Foundation: Comparative Worldview Curriculum, "trains elementary students to think biblically, exposes them to the basic beliefs of competing worldviews, and equips them with a framework through which they can filter every message, idea, and philosophy they encounter." [40]

During her presentation, she began with an overview of the rationale for worldview education and then walked the participants through an example of an activity related to the question, "What is truth?" I was impressed with how engaging and developmentally appropriate the lesson was. I learned, through experience, that in the same way we prepare lessons to teach the Bible, the lessons can and should also prepare students to think through the lens of a biblical worldview. An overview of my experience exemplifies the preparation of "worldview detectives."

The lesson was designed to enable students to "explain what it means for something to be true and defend why knowing and following the truth is or is not important."[41] The participants were divided into groups and asked what it means to tell the truth or think of times when they were asked to tell the truth. An interactive dialogue resulted in recording a definition, "truth is what is real" or something that really happened or was said.

This discussion was followed by an experience. Four groups were going to hunt for a hidden reward (chocolate). Each group received an envelope with instructions for where they would find the reward. However, only one set of instructions was correct and led the group to the reward. The other envelopes were misleading and led to a wrong place, or dead end, because the instructions did not line up with the truth or where the chocolate could actually be found. Each envelope had the name of the author of the instructions—Mrs. Reality, Mr. Intelligent, Miss Finish, and Mr. Mixture. Miss Finish's instructions were not complete, Mr. Intelligent's sounded good but were not based upon reality, and Mr. Mixture's were a bit of this and a bit of that, etc. Once the reward was discovered, the groups compared their instructions with those that came from Mrs. Reality. Participants were asked what they learned about the authors and their instructions and if having some instructions, regardless of source, was enough. It was concluded that unless you acted upon or followed the instructions based upon the truth, it would not lead to the chocolate.

The activity:

- Was designed with a defined outcome in mind
- Was engaging and involved collaboration
- Involved students in drawing their own conclusions
- Involved critical or evaluative thinking and data collection (detective skills)
- Involved the question of reality and its relationship to truth (worldview)

Extending Knowledge and Beliefs into Practice

When planning Bible instruction, be sure to imagine ways in which the children might respond. Guide them through the process of coming up with their own ideas. Think about your own response to the truth found within God's Word and be ready to share what you have already done, or will do, in response to God. Should the children not offer a response, then be ready to provide a suggestion.

During the weeks that follow, include opportunities for students to share their follow-through on their response plan. Did they follow up the lesson by acting upon their plan? What happened as a result of their obedience? Spiritual growth happens as students take truth to heart and, as a result, grow in their relationship with God. It is change that aligns with a biblical understanding of what it means to ***know.***

Contrasting Views of Learning: The Goal of Learning

Traditional Viewpoint (Greek and Roman):

a transfer of knowledge into the student

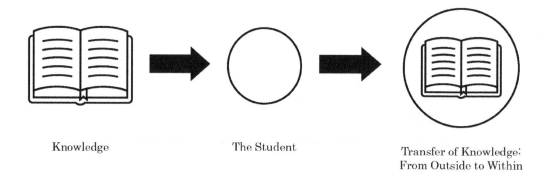

Knowledge   The Student   Transfer of Knowledge:
                                        From Outside to Within

The Biblical Viewpoint (Hebrew):

Knowledge is to be placed upon the heart;
the student when fully taught, becomes
the knowledge (knowing results in becoming)

- Emphasize that the Bible contains God's thoughts by using the example of evangelists like Billy Graham and David Jeremiah, who reminded and continued to remind listeners the truths being taught are from God. Throughout their teaching, they can be heard saying, "God says in the Bible that…"

- Do simple science experiments and predict what will happen. Explain that we can know or predict what will happen because of the creation laws (truths) that God created. For example, seeds can be planted, but it is God, through His design, that provides water through the rain, light from the sun, and nourishment through the soil. Through God's provision, He creates the flowers—all according to plan.

- Use science object lessons that allow you to easily teach the connection between nature's truth and God's truth. Always be sure to add life application teaching that guides children to answer questions such as, "What does this truth have to do with me?", "Why is this truth important?" and "What do I need to change in my life because of this truth?"

- Consider adding "who," "what," "where," "when," "why," and "how" questions to your lessons. These questions will automatically help your children to think through Scripture in a critical manner.

- On occasion, make statements like, "People are saying that we can do whatever we want to as long as most of the people would agree that it is OK." Follow the statement with, "Is this true?" It is important that they begin to understand that just because people agree with something, it does not make it true. Also ask, "How can we check to make sure that something is true?"

- Provide a truth board. This bulletin board should post, in addition to a current memory verse, an additional statement of truth. Ideally, locate this board where parents, in their coming and going, are likewise exposed to God's Word and also have the opportunity to know and support what the children are being taught. If teaching in a culturally diverse classroom, post verses not only in English but also in the "heart" (or first) language of the children and their parents.

- Use catechism questions and answers to teach Scripture and truth. Check out The New City Catechism and their free app.[42]

- Memorize what the Bible says about truth. See Appendix E for suggested verses.

- Children's worship songs can be integrated into Bible lessons and times of worship.
    - Check out the DLTK Bible website for a list of songs and poems about the Bible.[43]
    - The Bible (Mary Rice Hopkins)
    - Psalm 119:105-112 (Your Word) by JumpStart3
    - Hebrews 4:12 (Alive and Active) by JmpStart3
    - Psalm 119:18 (Open My Eyes) by JumpStart3
    - 2 Timothy 3:16 (All Scripture is Useful) by JumpStart3
    - "Speak, Oh Lord" by Keith and Kristyn Getty
    - "Word of God Speak" by Mercy Me
    - "Ancient Words" by Lynn Deshazo, sung by Michael W. Smith
    - "Thy Word" by Amy Grant
    - "Living Word" by Jeremy Camp
    - "The Word of God Has Spoken" by Travis Cottrell
    - "Your Words" by Third Day
    - "Order My Steps in Your Word" – African spiritual

- Learn the words to classic hymns that focus on truth.
    - "Ancient Words"
    - "God Has Spoken"
    - "The Truth of God Is Greater"
    - "The Word of God"
    - "Your Sovereign Word" [44]
    - "How Firm a Foundation"
    - "Standing on the Promises of God"

Reflect and Respond

1. In what specific ways are you modeling the importance of the Word of God within your ministry area?

2. Think about your recent Bible lessons. How much effort did you put forth to prepare for teaching the children? Did you take time to study God's Word?

3. Reflect upon your recent Bible lessons. Identify the responses children made to God's Word.

4. How could the understandings and suggestions within this chapter lay the foundation for a child's later understanding of the statement, "Truth from a biblical perspective is objective as opposed to subjective."

5. How can you effectively add questions to your next Bible lesson? Write them out and think through possible answers your children might give, including incorrect ones. Then, brainstorm ways you can guide them to true answers, so you will be ready to teach.

Chapter Five

Worldview Integration: Value

"Now this is the commandment, the statutes and the judgments which the LORD *your God has commanded me to teach you, that you might do them in the land where you are going over to possess it, ² so that you and your son and your grandson might fear the* LORD *your God, to keep all His statutes and His commandments which I command you, all the days of your life, and that your days may be prolonged. ³ O Israel, you should listen and be careful to do it, that it may be well with you and that you may multiply greatly..."*

Deuteronomy 6: 1-3a

"Blessed are those whose way is blameless, who walk in the law of the Lord! Blessed are those who keep His testimonies, who seek Him with their whole heart, who also do no wrong, but walk in His ways! You have commanded your precepts to be kept diligently. Oh, that my ways may be steadfast in keeping your statutes!"

Psalm 119:176 (ESV)

"Children obey your parents in the Lord for this is right. *"Honor your father and mother,"* which is the first commandment accompanied by a promise, namely, *"that it may go well with you and that you will live a long time on the Earth."*

Ephesians 6:1-3

Spiritual formation, as defined by Dallas Theological Seminary, is

> "The process by which God forms Christ's character in believers by the ministry of the Spirit, in the context of community, and in accordance with biblical standards."[45] This definition refers to a process that can and should begin in childhood and defines the goal as having the character of Christ in accordance with biblical values or standards.

It also addresses the need for the work of the Spirit, which aligns with the importance of leading a child to Christ as essential to beginning the process of spiritual formation.

The Bible, however, indicates a need to begin spiritual instruction prior to new birth. Parents, and teachers, are to place God's statutes upon their hearts, obey these commands, and then "diligently" teach them to their sons and daughters.

> In other words, the children were to be given concrete examples or models and 24/7 instruction (Deuteronomy 6:4-9).

Morality and character are aspects of axiology, or the study of values, and address questions like:

- What is of value, and how can we know what is right and wrong?
- What constitutes good and bad character?
- Who decides what is of value and beautiful?
- Are values objective or subjective?

The Bible also speaks to addressing the heart as the source of one's behavior (Mark 7:21), along with the motivation for choosing right over wrong—the fear of the Lord (Proverbs 1:7). God values the spiritual as opposed to the material and that which is eternal vs. the temporal (2 Corinthians 4:18).

Since man is made in the image of God and God called it good (Genesis 1:26-27), his total person is of value. He has a moral nature and knows right from wrong (conscience).[46] Being made in the image of a relational God, relationship with Him and others is of greatest importance or value. Sin has a direct impact on values—morality, ethics, and beauty. Because of sin, people value self over God and personal desires over God's will and purposes.

> Worldviews that exclude God at the center end up valuing self-fulfillment, autonomy, happiness, material things, position, power, and security. This shift is reflected in children who have too often been placed upon pedestals and overindulged in order to ensure their happiness.

In 1999, Charles Colson and Nancy Pearcy sounded an alarm when they wrote that Americans:

> "…have reached the 'modernist impasse.' They have been told that they had a right to be free from the restrictions of morality and religion, yet as unrestricted choices have led to social breakdown, they have begun to long for the protection that morality once provided."[47]

Fast forward to the present. What might be said of the current state of morality or relationship to authority and one another? I believe we are experiencing an even greater disrespect for authority and concern for one another. I recall, for example, an interviewee's response to why he was not wearing a mask or heeding social distancing during the COVID-19 epidemic: "I will be all right, and I really don't care about its effect on others." In light of the fact that the values and attitudes that will govern behavior in 2040 are presently being established in the mind and hearts of the next generation, the "modernist impasse" must be presently addressed and broken down within our classrooms.

Gene Garrick provides a summary of the biblical alternative and the thinking of a Christ-centered worldview[48]:

- **The possession of true life through sharing the life of God.** This was expressed by Jesus when He said, "What does it profit a man to gain the whole world and lose his own soul?" Redemption is to be valued above education.
- **Doing the will of God.** The world passes away, but he who does the will of God abides forever (1 John 2:15-17).

- **Obeying the law of God.** The law provides absolutes for behavior. These absolutes are not relative or subject to a majority vote (Matthew 5:17-19).
- **Sharing the love of God.** Once God's love has been received, it is then to be given back to God and others (Mark 12:30).
- **Thinking the thoughts of God.** God's thoughts, which are higher than ours, contain the beauty of life. Beauty is found in what is "true, honorable, right, pure, lovely, of good repute, excellent, worthy of praise" (Philippians 4:8).

Responding to Questions Regarding Value

What is of value?

Knowing God and belonging to Him is worth more than anything else in life. If we belong to Him, He wants us to think what He thinks, want what He wants, and do what He would have us do. The things of greatest value are related to God and His Kingdom, which He tells us to treasure more than the things on this Earth (Matthew 6:33).

> "Teacher, which commandment in the law is the greatest?" Jesus[b] said to him, *"'Love[c] the Lord your God with all your heart, with all your soul, and with all your mind.'*[d] This is the first and greatest[e] commandment. The second is like it: *'Love your neighbor as yourself.'*[f] All the law and the prophets depend[g] on these two commandments."
>
> Matthew 22:36-30 (NET)

What is right and wrong?
Who decides and how can we know?

God decides and has communicated the differences between right and wrong. When reading the Bible, we form our values and character by paying attention to His "lists" of what is right (wisdom from above) and wrong (earthly wisdom). Here is an example:

> Who is wise and understanding among you? By his good conduct, he should show his works done in the gentleness that wisdom brings. But

if you have bitter jealousy and selfishness in your hearts, do not boast and tell lies against the truth. [15] Such wisdom does not come from above but is earthly, natural, demonic. For where there are jealousy and selfishness, there is disorder and every evil practice. But the wisdom from above is first pure, then peaceable, gentle, accommodating, full of mercy and good fruit, impartial, and not hypocritical. And the fruit that consists of righteousness is planted in peace among those who make peace.

James 3:13-18 (NET)

He gave us the Ten Commandments and other direct statements that reveal God's values. He also shows us examples of people's right and wrong behavior in Bible stories. Man's ways are often sinful, but God's laws are right and for our good and our protection. God also taught His people through the Gospels and letters to the church within the New Testament. You too can read these letters and discover additional items for your list of what God does and does not value.

Do the rules (moral values and ethical standards) of right and wrong change?

God has not changed. He is Holy and good all of the time. His desire for us to love Him and follow Him has not changed. The truths found in the Bible likewise remain unchanged. They are based upon truth and God's desire for what is best for people. The values found in the Bible are objective and not subjective or based upon people's thinking and opinions. People may want to make changes to His laws, but, like God, His values endure forever.

Why should we follow God's rules?

He showed us how to live well because He loves us and wants what is best for us. He desires us to live in *shalom* (the way things should be). He created in each person the ability to make choices. We do not obey so that God will love us, but we obey because He has already loved us, and we love Him. When we follow His way, we fulfill God's chief purpose for our lives. We glorify Him and not ourselves.

Charles Colson, in his book *The Christian in Today's Culture,* wrote that our culture as a whole is doubleminded when addressing values. They have adopted a fact/value distinction. They believe:

> ...that science uncovers "facts" which they believe to be reliable and true, while morality and religion are based on "values," which they believe to be subjective and relative to the individual. Unfortunately, Christians often mirror this secular attitude. We tend to be confident about God's laws for nature, such as the laws of gravity, motion, and heredity; but we seem far less confident about God's laws for the family, education, or the state. *Yet a truly Christian worldview draws no such distinction. It insists that God's laws govern all creation.*[49]

John 1:3 states that "Through Him (Jesus) all things were made, without Him nothing was made that has been made." If Jesus made all things, then "all things" encompasses not just the design or laws of nature, but also a design for all aspects of life, including how people are to live and relate to one another—moral law and values.[50]

Other Worldviews: truth

The Question	Naturalism	Humanism	Pantheism
What is of value? Is there a moral code that defines right and wrong? Who or what decides?	The laws of nature, as defined by the scientific method, are the only source of laws that are absolute.	Values, morals, and right and wrong are defined by man's rational reasoning—both independently and collectively by society.	Found within the cosmos. Available through mystical consciousness and meditation.

Character Development: Pre-Operational Stage

Morality has both a cognitive and affective, or social, component. Moral theorist Lawrence Kohlberg applied Piaget's cognitive stages to moral thinking as the basis for his three stages of moral development.[51] Within each stage, there are two developmental levels.

The pre-conventional stage and the emergence of the first level of stage two, the conventional stage, most often occur during the early childhood years.[52] They are reviewed here since many children in third through fifth grade may still be operating within these stages. In reality, there are many adults whose moral development has not matured beyond the first level. Since young children are concrete and fundamental in their thinking and learning, decisions of what to do, or a right vs. wrong choice, are directly tied to the child's perceptions of the consequences.

> During early stage one, one is primarily motivated by a fear of punishment. The need for parental discipline and childhood obedience is thus emphasized by God in Scripture (Hebrews 12:5-6).

William Damon believes that the child's relationship to authority is the "most important moral legacy" handed down by parents.[53] I have previously summarized Damon's characteristics of authoritative parents (and teachers) as those who:

> *Consistently enforce behavioral expectations, showing a commitment to their importance. Their commands are direct and honest, not indirect and manipulative. They value obedience and associate good behavior with compliance with legitimate authority, and they confront children explicitly about any action that may harm (or negatively) impact others.*

In addition, Damon views induction as the most effective method of transmitting values. Induction is a technique for "ensuring the child's compliance through some form of control but, at the same time, drawing the child's attention to the reasons behind the standard."[54]

During the second phase of stage one, motivation shifts from avoiding punishment to seeking a reward. Individuals now consider the positives that result from right behavior.

> Throughout this phase, both cognitive and moral thinking is egocentric. The focus of one's thinking is on "What will happen to me?" Even doing something for someone else, especially during childhood, is likely a result of an anticipated reward as opposed to being motivated by other-directedness.

Empathy, or understanding the perspective of another, is not yet fully present due to the cognitive limitations of preoperational and early concrete operational thought. What may appear to be empathy on the part of a student may be a learned response to a stimulus within the context of their own past experiences and, in this sense, egocentric. Perhaps, some people well beyond childhood, due to a lack of nurture, have not developed empathy, as well.

In the case of children prior to the development of empathy, they may be imitating the response an adult has made during a similar circumstance or a response they might desire for themselves in the same situation.

> This points to the impact of imitation and modeling, but it likely does not, from a developmental perspective, reflect a response based upon other-directedness or a heart response.

Right behavior is being learned, and behaviors or habits, regardless of the level of understanding, are the beginning of character in children.

Character Development: The Conventional Level of Stage Two

Early spiritual development is directly related to the conventional level of moral thinking. Readiness for the Gospel message involves an understanding of sin and that a consequence of sin is punishment.

Unless the child has experienced authoritative (love balanced with control) discipline, the understanding that a holy God must punish sin is not understood and the need for a Savior, who takes the punishment in his or her stead, is likewise not understood.

> The appeal of Heaven as a reward for righteousness aligns with this thinking. Consider John 3:16 in this light. "For God so loved the world that He gave His only begotten Son, that whosoever believes in Him should not perish *[punishment]* but have everlasting life *[reward]*."

This is often the initial motivation for response to the Gospel. It does not downplay the validity of the decision but shows an important link between moral thinking and spiritual formation. It points to the importance of classroom discipline, an understanding of the concept of sin, an acknowledgment that he or she has sinned, the recognition of and acceptance of Jesus as Savior, and the subsequent reward of forgiveness, new life, and an eternal home.

During the transition to concrete operations and the emergence of empathy in the child, more socio-centric behavior begins. A felt need to please and be accepted as a good boy or girl becomes a motivating factor. There are rules of belonging, and to be accepted, these rules are followed. This level of thinking is easily observed in fourth-sixth-grade students.

Even though there is a greater awareness of what others think, the motivation at this stage is, in the end, still self-serving. In spite of these limitations, the other-directed behaviors that characterize membership in the body of Christ can be taught and associated with belonging to God and the church. The child's desire to be viewed as good by others can be akin to God's wishes and that He, too, like parents, has the expectation of right behavior and is pleased by their obedience. Teachers must, however, caution against making a relationship with God dependent upon being a good boy or girl. The children must understand that Christ died for them while they were yet sinners (Romans 5:8) and that goodness is not a requirement for forgiveness.

> Right behavior must be emphasized as a thankful response to God's love for us as opposed to a means of earning God's love and favor.

Throughout childhood, teachers and volunteers must remember that children are dependent upon fundamental learning experiences. This relates to the importance of modeling as a primary instructional tool. Children learn how to treat others and live together by watching how parents, teachers, and those more morally mature than themselves live other-directed lives. The behaviors between parents and children, and teachers and students, are the primary moral lessons. Children are also observers of how teachers and volunteers within a church setting interact with one another. Robert Coles, in his book on moral intelligence, writes,

> *"Moral intelligence isn't acquired only by memorization of rules and regulations, by dint of abstract classroom discussion or kitchen compliance. We grow morally as a consequence of learning how to*

be with others, how to behave in this world, a learning prompted by taking to heart what we have seen and heard. The child is a witness; the child is an ever-attentive witness of grown-up morality—or lack thereof; the child looks and looks for cues as to how one ought to behave and finds them galore as we parents and teachers go about our lives, making choices, addressing people, showing in action our rock-bottom assumptions, desires, and values, and thereby telling those young observers more than we realize."[55]

Too often, character lessons within the Bible remain too abstract or removed from the child's world. As children begin to understand that Bible lessons should result in change and that changes are often linked to behavior and how they treat others, they are taking the initial steps toward Christian character.

> Children must not merely come to know or identify a character trait (often an abstract definition or verse) but what a person of character does (the concrete or experiential meaning).

The abstractions must be made meaningful by "converting nouns into verbs: tasks to accomplish, plans for action, to be followed by the actual work of doing" (16). This is what is meant by biblical application. For example, "Be kind and *compassionate* to one another" (Ephesians 4:32a). This mark of godly character must be translated or made concrete through the guidance of parents and teachers.

- What does a compassionate boy or girl do?
- What don't they do?

Compassionate children offer to help someone when they have fallen and are crying on the playground. They share their snack when someone has forgotten to bring one, and they want to help homeless people by bringing food during a collection for a local food bank. Those who are not compassionate laugh when someone falls, and they ignore the needs of others and don't offer to help. They may even make fun of or bully children in need because they are different than themselves.

Extending Knowledge and Beliefs into Practice

One's view of value affects all areas of education. There is no such thing as a value-free area of study. Biblical values, right and wrong, must be taught through the authoritative message of Scripture. Teaching, discipline, and modeling are the means of inculcating the tendency to act in accordance with God's moral law. Teachers must expose students to the good, limit exposure to evil, and teach principles of choice. Children must be encouraged to think about their choices according to God's revealed will and standard.

– H. Gene Garrick

- Be mindful of one's character and relationships when serving children. Regular personal reflection and subsequent changes in behavior are essential in light of the importance of modeling.

- Understand that you will make mistakes in front of children. They will recognize those mistakes, too. You might lose your temper. You might hurt the feelings of a child or treat a child unfairly. When you do, apologize. This humble act teaches children what they should do in similar circumstances.

- Accountability partners are helpful as a means of not only identifying blind spots but taking the steps that lead to change and growth in one's own character. As a church leader, consider having regular volunteer "meet-ups," so those working with children can form relationships with the other volunteers. This will help the volunteers hold each other accountable as they teach Scripture to children.

- Create moral communities where authoritative discipline is practiced. Authoritative discipline is characterized by correction grounded in or balanced with love. Identify a set of classroom rules that can be consistently monitored and responded to when both followed and neglected. This requires a minimal number of clearly understood things that should and should not characterize student behavior while participating in the children's ministry program.

• Spiritual formation and the work of children's ministry within the church are both taught by and supported by the parents through their modeling, instruction, and encouragement at home. Create a regular newsletter (email) or blog as a means of communicating the verbs that demonstrate or define the character traits being taught and emphasized while in church. Have quarterly "parent meet-ups" and bring in guest speakers or hold parent training on different topics. This will allow parents to learn from and form relationships with other parents. Students imitate not only their parents and teachers but also the relationships between the two.

• Share or emphasize Bible stories that exemplify both right and wrong behavioral choices and their consequences.

• Read and discuss children's literature and movies that emphasize character and provide opportunities to insert God's truth into follow-up conversations with the students. Some examples include:

  ○ Children's books related to character are readily available online and can be used to locate additional books related to a desired trait. One example is *Picture Books to Support Character Education*.[56] Keep in mind that not all picture books are for young children. As a matter of fact, most of Patricia Polacco's books, one of my favorite authors, are more appropriate for use among middle grades or even middle school students than with K-2 students. Some of her books where character (other-directedness) is a focus include:
    • *Chicken Sunday*
    • *Junkyard Wonders*
    • *Mrs. Katz and Tush*
    • *The Lemonade Club*
    • *Lube and the Wren*
    • *Something About Hensley's*
    • *Tucky Jo and Little Heart*
    • *Gifts of the Heart*
  ○ Newberry Award-winning books, geared toward upper grades by nature of content and reading levels, often open the door to worldview discussions (reality, nature of man, and values). Both protagonists and

antagonists exhibit values within the context of the stories. Consider starting a book club as a means of not only instruction geared toward worldview issues like character but also as a means of developing more time with students and playing "worldview detectives. Appendix D is a previously written article from "Make Way for Books"[57] discussing the use of Newberry books as a worldview teaching tool. Always read the books in advance and make note of whether or not the story is appropriate and also useful for a worldview discussion. Remember that all authors write from a worldview, whether or not they intend to. Ask students what they believe the author's worldview is. Ask them to read something from the book to defend their conclusion. Does the viewpoint or behavior of a character align with God's viewpoint in the Bible? No time for a book club? Share a selection from a familiar story, book, or movie, and have a similar discussion.

- Sections of movies can be used to discuss worldview and moral character. Be sure to watch them before you show them (bathroom humor will exist). Form questions that children can answer as you watch. *Please* be sure to follow copyright laws for use within classrooms. Examples are *Smallfoot, Frozen 2, Spider-Man: Into the Spider-Verse, Zootopia, Toy Story 4, Christopher Robin, Instant Family, Abominable, Finding Dory, Paddington 2, The Greatest Showman, Aladdin, Lego Batman, Wonder, Beauty and the Beast, Sing,* and *Despicable Me 3.*

- Provide opportunities for the children to serve others. Nursing home visitations and performances, collecting food for the hungry within the community, showing gratitude to first responders who serve areas near the church, picking up classroom trash, and wiping down tables at the end of the church program are some examples of other-directed behaviors. Also, consider family service opportunities where the children can work alongside their parents (e.g., community clean-up projects, yard care for the elderly, preparing gifts to distribute to children at Christmas).

- Have students examine (collaboratively) passages like Romans 12, 1 Thessalonians 4, and Philippians 2 for insights into behavior or values that should and should not characterize a follower of Jesus.

- Memorize Scripture that addresses values and character. See Appendix E.

- Children's songs related to value:

  - "Fruit of the Spirit" (Kids Spring Children's Ministry)
  - "The Perfect Ten" (Katie Hill)
  - "It Is Good" (Mary Rice Hopkins)
  - "Kindness" (Remba Kids)
  - "Wanna Be A Sheep" (Mary Rice Hopkins)
  - "Walk Like Jesus" (Mary Rice Hopkins)
  - "Sharing Comes 'Round Again" (Mary Rice Hopkins)
  - "God's Love" (Mary Rice Hopkins)
  - "John 9:5" (Light of the World) by JumpStart3
  - "John 15:5" (I am the Vine) by JumpStart3
  - "Romans 1:16" (I Am Not Ashamed of the Gospel) by JumpStart3
  - "Thankful" (Group Publishing)
  - "Faith" (Group Publishing)
  - "I Won't Be Afraid" (Group Publishing)
  - "Light of the World" (Group Publishing)
  - "Live Differently" (Yancy)
  - "Be Careful" (Yancy)
  - "Wanna Be Like Jesus" (Yancy)
  - "I'm Gonna Live So God Can Use Me" (African spiritual)
  - "Take Me to the Water" (African spiritual)

- Lead a worldview discussion: For example, open the discussion by reading Exodus 20:12 and continue by asking the questions, "Why do you think this command is directed to children? How does this passage relate to what we know about a Christian worldview?" If one is obedient within the home, respect and submission can be applied to one's relationship with God.

  - What must parents provide if children are to obey? Parents must exercise their authority and provide standards or rules.
  - How does this relate to our discussion?
  - How do the fruits of the Spirit fit into the picture?
  - Why do parents provide boundaries and rules? (Love, safety, training, so children will do well in life, etc.)
  - Read Proverbs 15:5 and Hebrews 12:11 or other verses related to discipline.

Reflect and Respond

What are the enduring ideas (ideas at the heart of the matter and instructional effectiveness) found within this chapter?

1. Brainstorm the character traits emphasized at each level of your children's ministry. Justify the reason the traits are biblical *and* developmentally appropriate for this age group. Consider creating a scope and sequence that would list traits that should be emphasized at each grade level. Include a memory verse for each trait. List what someone who demonstrates the trait would do and not do. Use examples provided by students past and present. This would make a great bulletin board!

2. Examine your attitude toward discipline. Do you view discipline as a distraction or as a means for spiritual formation? Is discipline within your classroom authoritarian or authoritative? What is the difference?

3. To what degree are the parents involved as members of your moral community? What can be done to increase their involvement? Research conducted by Christian Smith in 2005 on the spiritual lives of teens found that the primary influencer was the parent. He concluded that the teens were not as influenced by culture as one might think, but they were instead on track to become just like their parents.[58]

4. Reflect on the current effectiveness of your efforts toward moral and character development. What is the basis for your conclusion and how might you validate it?

Chapter Six

Worldview Integration: Humankind's Nature and Purpose

So, God created mankind in His own image, in the image of God He created them, male and female He created them.

Genesis 1:27

For all have sinned and fall short of the glory of God.

Romans 3:23

You have searched me, Lord, and you know me. ² You know when I sit and when I rise; you perceive my thoughts from afar. ³ You discern my going out and my lying down; you are familiar with all my ways.

Psalm 139:1-3

So, whether you eat or drink or whatever you do, do it all for the glory of God.

1 Corinthians 10:31

"Man cannot be defined adequately as an animal, or as a social being, nor even as a rational being. He must be defined as the whole that he is, a spirit or person, or self whose normal and ultimate end is fellowship with God in the ultimate society of the many bound into the One."[59]

J. Donald Butler

The questions related to the nature and purpose of humanity complete the basic philosophical or worldview questions. It is critical that children develop a proper understanding of the nature of men, women, boys, and girls for two primary reasons.

> The world presents an array of misconceptions during a time when children are developing their concept of self.

Secondly, an understanding of self and one's place in the family and community is a focus of social development and the realization of *shalom*—peace with God, others, and self.

Man, apart from the biblical perspective, is viewed as a "creature of biology."

> "Biological nature is human nature. Its conception of educational research is grounded in the faith that the scientific study of the human organism can give us all essential knowledge of human nature and behavior—that is, knowledge not simply of man's biophysiological equipment, but also of his basic needs and powers, his primary likes and aversions, his drives, his enduring interests, and his invariant principles of growth and learning."[60]

Psalm 8:3-6 presents the contrasting biblical viewpoint.

> *"When I consider Your heavens, the work of your fingers, the moon, and the stars, which you have set in place, what is man that you are mindful of him, the son of man that you care for him? You made Him a little lower than the heavenly beings and crowned Him with glory and honor. You made Him ruler over the works of your hands, you put everything under His feet."*

> A biblical worldview defines men, women, and children as different in kind from all other aspects of creation—animal, vegetable, and mineral.

People are the highest form of life made in the image of God (Genesis 1:26-27) with the ability to think, act on his or her own (free will), communicate, and organize. As an image-bearer, every individual is both a personal being with a mind, emotions, will, and conscience and a relational being capable of fellowship with God and family.

As an image-bearer, men and women reflect God passively or involuntarily like all of creation, but they, as stewards of the mysteries of God (1 Corinthians 4:1), are also free to choose and glorify God voluntarily, do His will, and have fellowship with Him.[61]

The image and nature of humans have been marred because of sin. Everyone has been given the ability to freely choose, but man did not obey God or choose to image Him. As a result, fellowship with God was broken.

> Instead of a life centered upon God's will and His purposes for life, the focus shifted to self and life independent from God.

Consequently, because of sin, people are born with deceitful and wicked hearts (Jeremiah 17:9). In spite of man's fallen nature, Scripture still refers to man as made in God's image (1 Cor. 11:7, James 3:9) because "he [or she] still has responsibility as God's image-bearer and still retains his personhood in God's likeness...even though he has lost the image in his purpose."[62]

Only God Himself can resolve the conflict between man as an image-bearer and as a sinner. It is not education alone that can address the problem and improve a man or woman's condition, but it is the restoration of man's relationship with God that is needed.

> Salvation is, therefore, the foundation for spiritual growth and should be viewed as a critical spiritual outcome within the children's ministry across all levels.

Responding to Questions Regarding Man

Where did we come from?

The Bible says that the first man and woman were created from the dust of the ground and that it was God who breathed life into them.

What are men and women like? How are they different from the rest of the things that God created?

People were created in the image of God. They are different from all the other things that God created. They can think, solve problems, be creative, and use a language to communicate with each other and with God. As image-bearers, we share many attributes with God: "...humans are persons who can think, who experience joy and sorrow, who make choices, who are self-aware, and who communicate, covenant, and love. The God who exists possesses all these abilities, as well.[63] Robert Ferris discusses ways in which humankind is both like and unlike God:

- Is real as opposed to idols, which are not real
- Can know and think (intellect)
- Experiences emotions
- Has a will and makes choices
- Is self-aware or knows their own thoughts
- Can experience relationships with others and within the Trinity
- Communicates
- Makes commitments or promises[64]

God is at the same time so different that we cannot fully understand or comprehend what He is like. He knows all things; He is always present; He is one God but three persons and can create something from nothing. He can "change physical realities [*perform miracles*] in order to achieve His purposes and to protect His people" (20).

> The Bible says that each person is "wonderfully made" and known by God from the time they start to grow within their mother.

Each person is different. They look and behave differently, but they all are equally important because they were all created by God to reflect Him. Each person even has a unique fingerprint. Each person has been given special talents and ways of thinking.

Why do people do bad things?

God gave people the ability to make choices. They are not like robots. They make choices about what they can and will do. They also decide what they do not want to do. Satan tempted Adam and Eve, the first man and woman, to not listen to or obey God. They chose to disobey God and have their own way. This wrong choice caused them to be separated from God.

Because of disobedience, sin entered God's created world, and all people have had a sinful nature and sinned ever since. It is because of sin people make self-centered, wrong choices and do bad things. It is because of sin people die.

How does someone become a good person?

God loves all people, but people choose to disobey God. Because God loves His creation and especially people, He had a plan to deal with sin and restore relationships with people. This is good news, and this good news is called the Gospel. God sent His Son, Jesus, to be punished for the sins of people. Since the punishment for sin is death, Jesus took our place and died for us on the cross. God offers people forgiveness as a gift. People cannot earn forgiveness, but they can repent (confess) and accept the gift by believing what God did when Jesus died for them. When people accept this gift or offer of forgiveness, the Bible tells us that they are made new. It is like being born again. Their sins are forgiven, and they are now a new creation and seen again as perfect in the eyes of God.

What does it mean to be a "new creation"?

After repentance and receiving the gift of salvation through God's grace, the Bible says that our old ways, which were influenced by sin, are past, and our lives have been made new in and through Jesus Christ. Whereas we used to be controlled by sin, or what the Bible refers to as "the flesh," the believer now has the Holy Spirit in his or her life. All believers receive the Holy Spirit. Before receiving the Holy Spirit, we were likely to rebel against God, want our way instead of God's way, not acknowledge our sin, and reject His gift of salvation through grace. The Spirit helps us desire and understand God's Word. Sin is now acknowledged, and we trust God and have a desire to follow Him. We also want to serve others and be His witnesses. The Holy Spirit gives power and strength we did not have before. Our character, or behavior, can reflect God as we choose to daily "walk" in step with the Spirit through the Spirit's gifts to us—love, joy, peace, patience, kindness, goodness, faithfulness, gentleness, and self-control.

What does God want His people and children to do?

God wants all people to know, love, worship, and serve Him. He wants them to love and care for others and tell them about God and His Son Jesus. The New Testament was written to tell people how they should and can live so that others see an example of what God is like. He wants people to not only know His Word but also share what they learn with others.

What happens when someone dies?

People who repent and trust in Jesus to forgive their sins go to Heaven and live with Him forever. People who rebel against God, and who have not been forgiven, will be punished for their sins when they die.

Other Worldviews: truth

The Question	Naturalism	Humanism	Pantheism
Who is humankind: men, women, boys, and girls?	Most advanced or highly evolved animal	Highly evolved and advancing or evolving through their rational potential, problem-solving, and inventive abilities	Human beings are impersonal, spiritual beings who are God
What are humankind's nature and needs?	Matter: A blend of chemical and physical properties	Naturally good, autonomous and capable of self-fulfillment	Divine like all aspects of the cosmos

A Student-Sensitive, Student-Directed Orientation

An understanding of boys and girls must be at the heart of the teaching and learning process. Volunteers and Bible teachers are teaching children and not curriculum. A curriculum is a means to the end, but it is the students who do the work of learning.

At a parenting conference in Virginia Beach, VA, in 1976, I (Milt) was introduced to what would become a ministry life verse—Psalm 139:3. The speaker was "Buck"

Hatch from Columbia Bible College, now Columbia International University. He asked the audience of young parents some questions:

> "How many of you are here because you want to be the best parents possible?"

> "How many of you are willing to consider parenting your children the way your heavenly Father parents you?"

He proceeded to explain what he believed was the biblical starting point. Parents must become "intimately acquainted" (Psalm 139:3) with each child, their ways, their thinking, their talents, their temperaments, their developmental timeline, etc. Not only must one become acquainted with the child's ways during their current stage of development, but also their ways along the continuum of development—infancy, early childhood, childhood, preadolescence, adolescence, and young adulthood.[65] (See Appendix B.[66])

> It was at that point that I caught the vision to get to know my children but also the children I was to teach and lead. Too often, teachers study curriculum, discipline, and instructional strategies without ever becoming students of their students.

Children are viewed as immature in Scripture. They must be taught everything, and their primary instructional mode is firsthand experience and interactive dialogue (talk and discussion).

Paul in his letter to the Corinthians refers to a child's cognitive differences by saying that children "speak like a child, think like a child, and reason like a child" (1 Cor. 13:11). They grasp parts, but it is not until later that they can see more clearly, make connections, or form concepts. It is the ability to form concepts that opens a window to understanding basic theological ideas.

Worldview truths often remain abstract because the language surrounding the ideas has little or no experiential basis. Teachers must, therefore, keep in mind that worldview is being laid through what is experienced as opposed to direct instruction (lecture). It is teacher talk based upon or during firsthand experiences that provides meaning. Reflect on Deuteronomy 6.

Whilhoit and Dettoni, when writing on the developmental (or child-directed) perspective, refer to active learning as an asset.

> Knowledge is constructed during those interactive moments between mental processing and environmental intrusion. This includes more than telling. If the teacher is reading or speaking, the learner must be given something to actively listen for or recognize. It suggests hands-on, try out, experiment, fit to your situation, build on your experience methodology. It means we cannot substitute formulas or just words for understanding.[67]

It is also important to remember that during grades three through six, students' language and reading abilities vary greatly. They may struggle when needing to express ideas verbally and when being asked to read for information or out loud before their peers. This variance can be mistaken for lack of interest and may become the cause as to why children who struggle do not want to attend Sunday school. By nature, children, and even adults for that matter, avoid stressful situations and being embarrassed in front of peers. Children will even "clown" or be disruptive because it is better to be laughed at or corrected for intentional behaviors than to be embarrassed for not knowing the answer or their inability to read. For this reason, children should be cautiously called upon to recite or read before an audience unless they volunteer or you are confident they are ready and able. Failure within any context can be interpreted by children as "not belonging" and a belief that one does not belong will threaten a child's sense of safety within the church context.

Elementary-age children are also, by nature, still dependent. They know that they cannot make it on their own, and they look to parents and other care providers to meet their needs. Their dependence leads to a "faith" in their parents' provision. Scripture refers to the child's humility and trust as a model. It is not the child that should model the adult, but the adult that should be like a child (Matthew 18:3-4).

Teachers, through relationships with their students, can guide their students in transferring their trust and faith to God, the one who unconditionally loves them and will always care for them. **There should be a sense of urgency in that, once students reach the preteen years, when independence is increasingly asserted, this transfer becomes more difficult.**

Teaching must strive to develop the student's potential as an image-bearer. Their innate or God-designed potential must be recognized and encouraged. Provide opportunities for each student to use their talents within the classroom and in service to others. Upon conversion, a student's spiritual gifts should begin to emerge and likewise be given opportunity to flourish.

Classroom experiences sometimes uncover tasks that may, for some, be more difficult. They must come to know that "being average" or, in some cases below average, in some areas is acceptable. In so doing, they will realize not just the truths concerning all persons, but also a knowledge of themselves.[68] A child's belief about self and their abilities are directly related to what they can and cannot do. An "I can't" or "I'm not good enough" attitude can mar the child's self-confidence and ability to persevere and pursue all that God has designed for them.

Extending Knowledge and Beliefs into Practice

- Commit to becoming a student of your students and to providing experiences that are developmentally appropriate or student-directed. You may want to begin by referring to Appendix A: Developmental Theories with Relevance to Spiritual Development.[69]

- Lead parents in having an honest understanding of their child's talents and abilities. Encourage the acknowledgment of their child's talent but likewise help them accept areas where their child is average. Help parents also understand that struggles are character-building opportunities

- If possible, in your ministry context, incorporate home visits and family picnics to get to know children and their backgrounds. Ask parents to tell you about their student's likes, dislikes, and talents, etc.

- If ethnic and cultural diversity characterize your ministry, then study the cultures and ways of thinking of students who are not from your background. Always be mindful of the social norms within a culture when interacting with children and their families. All children must experience a sense of belonging.

- Avoid an overemphasis on "empty" praise. The words "good job," for example, lose meaning through overuse and more so when it is used to describe something that does not deserve it. Sometimes, the words "good effort" are the more appropriate statement. Shift attention from the end product to the process.

- Involve the children in developmentally appropriate service projects within the church and community. Create "homeless bags" that children can keep in a parent's car to give to someone on the side of the road; have a trash day to scour the church grounds for trash clean-up. Invite families to share needs that might be in their neighborhoods, like raking leaves or spreading mulch, and coordinate a family service day.

- Create a mentoring program at your church, which will allow children to learn and experience how to help run sound and lights, take up an offering, work in the nursery, play an instrument in the orchestra, or sing on the worship team. Remember, our purpose is not to have perfect worship services but raise a generation of children who feel like they belong in the church. Christian Smith found a church that accepts and involves students as a vital part of the congregation to be a common factor among teens who were growing in their faith.[70]

- Share children's literature that tells the stories of children who have overcome difficulties and followed and achieved their dreams.

- Start to develop the purpose of learning as preparation for what God asks them to do as opposed to being able to merely recall information.

- Integrate Bible stories that can be used to emphasize that God has a plan for each of His children. Rick Warren, the author of the *Purpose Driven Life*, has created a storybook Bible using stories that emphasize how God wants us to live and a desire to help children discover God's plan for their lives. Each of the stories concludes with a biblical truth, a verse to remember, and an application question. Many of the stories would likewise help in developing a biblical view of value.[71]

- See Appendix E for memory verses that relate to the nature of men, women, boys, and girls.

Reflect and Respond

1. According to this chapter, why is it important for children to have a biblical understanding of self?

2. Once you understand the different philosophies of self, you will hear examples of them everywhere. What was something you heard or saw that exemplified an unbiblical philosophy of self? What does the Bible say, instead?

3. How does understanding child development help you teach faith foundations?

4. What experiences do you offer in your Bible classroom or children's ministry that help children learn about themselves and others? What can you do to improve?

Chapter Seven

The Redemptive Story

*According to the grace of God given to me, like a skilled master-builder,
I laid a foundation, but someone else builds on it. And each one must
be careful how he builds. ¹¹ For no one can lay any foundation other
than what is being laid, which is Jesus Christ.*

1 Corinthians 3:10-11

So, faith comes from hearing and hearing through the Word of God.

Romans 10:17

*And that from childhood you have known the sacred writings which
are able to give you the wisdom that leads to salvation through faith
which is in Christ Jesus.*

2 Timothy 3:15 (NASB)

*What then is necessary for child conversion? The same thing that
is essential in adult conversion: a conscious turning from sin and a
turning toward God...Incline the child to put his faith in Christ by
sound Christian teaching surrounded by Christian love from birth
onward. Such pre-evangelism, as it may be called, builds a proper
foundation for intelligent faith and active discipleship.*

Edward L. Hayes[72]

Parents want the best possible future for their children, so they seek the "right" educational experiences as a means to future success. This desire reflects "the pattern of this world" or the culture in which we live. In the midst of their searching, the importance of the church's children's ministry may be overlooked due to a failure to think from the perspective of a Christ-centered worldview. However, their children's future, apart from a Christ-centered perspective, lacks meaning, purpose, and joy both now throughout eternity. What could be more important than that?

The lack of ethics and moral code within culture also means that some attendees (seekers) within churches are motivated by a desire for character education. They perceive that public education fails to adequately meet this need, so they look to a church and memories of Sunday school to address this need. They rightly understand that the Bible addresses character along with right and wrong behavior, but what they fail to realize is that their child's needs, rooted in a fallen nature and self-centered worldview, cannot be met through moral teaching alone. The children's ministry must embrace the opportunity to not only impact a child's character but also address the deeper need—new life in Jesus.

Ted Tripp in *Shepherding a Child's Heart* points out that the orientation of a child's heart will be influenced to go in one of two directions. It will be directed either Godward or toward "things that are not God and that cannot satisfy."[73] He says, "Children are either growing in their understanding of the implications of who God is, or they are seeking to make sense of life without a relationship with God...The question is not 'will they worship?'; it is always 'Whom will they worship?'" (22).

The answer to the question, "What will the children choose to do about Christ?" is the essential question. In the same way that there is no neutral education, there is no neutrality when it comes to Jesus. The children will either come to know and follow Him or continue to go their own way. The choice to believe in Jesus is the first and most foundational steppingstone along the path of spiritual growth and formation. It is for this reason that children's ministry leaders must understand and provide the means to that first step—the Gospel of Jesus Christ.

The Christian Worldview Narrative

Children prior to the upper elementary grades are egocentric and see life only from their perspective. This is not because they are self-centered, but because the ability to see things from another's perspective has not yet developed. However, it does, unless otherwise directed, naturally develop into self-centeredness. Elementary level ministry has the opportunity to focus the child's attention beyond themselves to God and others---from a narrow perspective to the grand narrative.

> Through instruction and modeling, the children must be introduced
> not only to the story but to the idea that they are part of that story.

All worldviews have a narrative. Valid worldviews have not only a story, but a story that provides a meaning and purpose for life. The story must be logical, consistent and worthy of placing one's faith in it. It must work. The biblical narrative is the only one, that upon close examination, meets the criteria.[74]

God's story is the basis for all other good stories. Stories contain the classic five acts, as illustrated by Shakespeare's plays. "Listen in" as Lawrence and Nancy Goldstone discuss the story with children:[75]

> "Shakespeare uses the first act," we say, "to introduce his characters,
> and then, in the second act, he throws them together and lets the conflict
> build. In the third act, the conflict boils over, the climax is reached,
> and the protagonist (and often the antagonist) is changed forever. In
> the fourth act, we see the impact of the climax on the characters, and
> in the fifth act, we find out what happens to everyone." (60)

The Goldstones also identify the protagonist as the character in the story who is "trying to push the action forward," while the antagonist, a person or idea, tries to "hold the action back." This pushing backward and forward creates a conflict. When you identify these elements, you "have come a long way to knowing what the story is about" (26).

The story of God and His purpose for humans to reflect Him and fill the Earth with His glory has all of the components.

God had a plan to create man and enter into a relationship with Him (creation). God created humans as unique reflections of His glory and commissioned them to "be fruitful and multiply" and thus reflect His glory throughout the Earth.

Satan, the antagonist, seeks to destroy God's plan and persistently tempts humans to rebel and abandon God's purpose for their lives through disobedience. The result is humans experience the consequences of their sin and live in separation from knowing and having fellowship with God and others (the fall).

God, through His love and grace, revealed a plan to redeem lost sinners and bring them back to Himself. The struggle between those who are living for the glory of God and those who are not unfolds across time. Humans constantly turn their backs on God and experience the consequences of going their own way, while God continually demonstrates grace and mercy and invites humans to repent and return to Him.

The story climaxes when Jesus, the centerpiece of God's plan, comes to perfectly reflect the glory of God while humbling Himself and offering His life to redeem those living in rebellion to God and His purpose. This act of love culminates with Jesus' resurrection and victory over sin and death. The story continues as the impact of Jesus' life and death unfolds in the book of Acts and the Epistles and as the apostles take the good news of the resurrection throughout the world.

These ambassadors of the good news not only invite people to return to a restored relationship with God and His purpose for their lives but to complete the original purpose of God for humans to fill the Earth with the reflection of His glory, both individually and through the church.

When people understand their invitation to participate in God's purpose for their lives, they realize that the story includes them and that they can have a special part in God's ongoing story. The story of God promises that His purposes will be achieved and foretells our relationship with Him throughout eternity.

Teaching "One Story"

Barna has concluded that there are four "cornerstones" related to the formation of a spiritual champion.[76] The second cornerstone is a "commanding knowledge of biblical content," and cornerstone three is "the identification of organizing principles." Knowledge of the one story does not only satisfy the need for knowledge, *but it is also a framework for organizing that knowledge.*

> It provides a means of taking the parts of the story, too often taught in isolation and out of sequence, and integrating them into a meaningful whole.

Ed Stetzer, in a *Christianity Today* article, expresses a concern that grows, in part, out of the fear that the Bible can become a group of "isolated morality tales, like Aesop's Fables."[77]

> This teaching too often merely results in a model for right living based on good and bad behavior as opposed to the telling of the bigger story that forms the basis for teaching the Gospel.

Stetzer goes on to state that children can miss the "plan that has been designed and implemented by a loving God for the saving of humans." Stetzer explains:

> ...we hear Jesus say in 1 Corinthians 11, 'This cup is the New Covenant in My blood. Do this as often as you drink it in remembrance of Me.' However, we don't remember that Moses said, 'This blood is a symbol of the covenant' in the Old Testament. We don't understand why Abraham would be called to sacrifice Isaac if we don't understand what would happen as God the Son is sent by God the Father to be the perfect sacrifice for our sins. This interconnectedness happens throughout Scripture.

It is not uncommon to find teachers who are either not familiar with the full plot of Scripture and how the entire story fits together from beginning to end. As a result, the Bible is often viewed through the limited lens of historical stories or as a handbook limited to the instructions for our salvation. Without understanding the full story, we miss the revelation of God's purpose for creation and our purpose within the greater context of the revelation of His glory.

The full plot of Scripture, the one story, is revealed through two acts. Each act contains seven scenes. The first act begins by introducing us to the Mission of God and ends in failure with 400 years of unrest and silence. Act II, begins by informing us that God is committed to fulfilling His mission and ends with victory, and eternal shalom.

Because it is crucial for both students and teachers to see and comprehend the whole story as opposed to disintegrated or disconnected parts, the next book within the Distinctively Christian Series will be devoted to how to understand and teach this single story while recognizing the scenes and the unifying themes or threads that are found throughout the Bible; including the unifying themes of God's glory, reconciliation and atonement, and the revelation of The Kingdom of God.

Preparation for the Gospel

Spiritual growth is directly related to how an individual understands and responds to the Word of God.[78]

It is the Holy Spirit that prepares hearts, and God uses teachers in the process of equipping the student to hear, understand, and respond to the Word of God[79]. The teacher prepares the soil upon which the seed will be planted. Much of this book has been devoted to understanding the necessary "nutrients" within a rich soil. Enriched soil allows children to understand and connect with the message.

Browne outlines six types of soil that can be aligned with his six stages of faith. His explanation, defined by Scripture, outlines the barriers to faith as well as the spiritual needs that characterize each stage. These stages are not age-specific, and therefore, individual children within a group may be at different levels (soil types) of growth on the skeptic to fisherman timeline.

STAGES OF SPIRITUAL GROWTH (Browne, 2012, p. 43-46)			
	Description of the heart	Invitation from Christ	Barriers to growth	Spiritual needs
Skeptic	Calloused heart, deaf ears, closed eyes	Repent, believe	Lack of spiritual understanding	Befriended by a loving and praying, believing friend. A personal change of mind and heart initiated by the Holy Spirit.
Seeker	Ready heart, open ears, questions	Repent, believe	Lack of clear presentation of the Gospel, lack of an invitation	Clear Gospel presentation and invitation to receive, believe.
Believer	Seed begins to germinate, shallow soil, little or no roots	Follow	Lack of root, testing, trouble, persecution,	Prayer, roots, knowledge, teaching, worship time, someone to walk with them.
Follower	Beginning to push through the soil and struggle with thorns	Deny self, pick up cross, trust, obey, love Christ and others	Thorns, worries of this life, doubt, deceitfulness of wealth, comfort, self	Deny self, trials, endurance, perseverance, time, small group relationships, and accountability
Friend	Good soil, obedient to Christ, fruit	Love, obey, go	Complacency, fear, pride, lack of vision, lack of equipping	Continued obedience. Equipping, empowerment, continued spurring, and accountability within a community
Fisherman	Good soil, fruit, harvest, influence, reflect Christ	Teach others	Complacency, fear, pride, lack of vision, lack of equipping, weariness	Perseverance, humility, faithfulness, accountability, reliable people

Children's ministry, regardless of the ages served, should include a focus on *evangelism readiness*. Evangelism readiness is the preparation of soil upon which the seed of the Gospel can be sown.

Donald Joy writes,

> "Early, consistent saturation in a warm, Christian nurture environment helps children respond personally to Christ's call to salvation…a child's need is for a warm identification environment in which he *or she* may develop a strong sense that he is loved by God and by the Christians around him."[80]

This supports the need for a living curriculum, as discussed in chapter two.

> In today's culture, there may be more skeptics within our early childhood and elementary ministries than ever before.

If you rewind to the earlier decades, you will find, with few exceptions, that children involved in children's ministry were from homes where a life of faith was modeled and taught. Children usually came from an environment where nurturing their child's faith was a priority. If we are honest, this priority, even in many Christian homes, has been replaced with "I just want my child to be happy!" Interestingly enough, instead of happiness, far too many children are experiencing stress, lack of resiliency, addiction to technology, limited self-help skills, and self-centeredness.

Secondly, even though children may not have had an early Christian nurturing, the parents, even though not Christian, were less likely to express bias against Christians and their beliefs. However, many of today's children may be experiencing negative comments regarding the Bible and the church within their homes and through media exposure. This may not be the case within the Christian home, but unchurched families who bring children to church for a few years of moral education may openly display negative attitudes and a personal lack of need for the church. Comments like, "I don't believe in God" or "The Bible is a bunch of make-believe stories" may not only be overheard but directed to children. Since children are imitators, they too may be more skeptical.

Ministry leaders need to keep in mind that in cases such as these, children are stuck in the middle. They love their parents but want to please their ministry leaders, too. Understanding that a child might feel confusion and anxiety because of this is a reality within ministry.

Thirdly, due to the increased frequency of verbal and physical abuse and neglect, the ability to trust may not be present.

> Take note of the spiritual needs of a skeptic: the need for a loving, believing, praying friend and an environment where the possibility of a change, through the working of the Holy Spirit, is a very real possibility.[81]

The seeker has moved beyond "closed ears and eyes" to being ready for a clear presentation of the Gospel and an invitation to believe. The context of the bigger redemptive story increases readiness to obey Jesus and follow Him. These new believers will find nurture for their tender roots in a distinctively Christian environment where teachers shepherd, worship, pray, teach, and encourage them to trust Jesus and allow Him to "be their boss."

Sharing the Gospel

The actual presentation of the Gospel should be at the child's level and taught in a simple, straightforward way. The language should align with the language of the Gospel repeated throughout the redemptive story. Use the phrase "The Bible says" not only within Bible stories but throughout the presentation of the Gospel, as well.

Share these truths:

- God loves you.
- He wants to be your friend (have a relationship with you), but all people have sinned and want their own way.
- It is because of God's love and grace that God sent His only son to Earth as a means of taking care of the sin problem.
- Christ died to take the consequences of your sin and provide a way your sins can be forgiven.

- Confess to God that you have sinned and ask for His forgiveness.
- Know that through His love and grace, God has forgiven you, and if you believe God will do what He has promised, then know that He also welcomes you as one of His children.

These basic elements are often taught through instructional tools like wordless books or bracelets. These and other Gospel tools help children link and remember the components of the Gospel. The language of the presentation should be culturally responsive. For example, depending on the ethnicity of students, the representation of the color black with sin and white with the absence of sin may lack sensitivity and hinder the responsiveness of the child. An alternative approach may be the substitution of the wordless book's black page with a smudged brown page and then, through the blood of Jesus, show a brown page without smudges. This approach does not use color as part of the presentation.

Consider the vocabulary that is used in presenting the Gospel. Ask yourself, do the children know the meaning of the words I am using? Have I used this vocabulary regularly within the context of my Bible teaching and within the redemptive narrative?

> Avoid the tendency to link being good boys and girls to being loved by God.

Children are surrounded by expectations to be good. "Good job" has become a sort of mantra over recent years. Yes, right behavior is God's desire, but it is not the basis of His love.

> Make sure that God's grace is understood throughout the redemptive story. All biblical characters were sinners and, as such, fell short. God, however, chose and welcomed them and used them within His plan.

Throughout the redemptive story, look for the grace and the foreshadowing of Jesus. Help children to understand the good news, "God demonstrates His own love for us, in that while we were still sinners, Christ died for us" (Romans 5:8). Bible teachers are God's mouthpiece, but teachers are not the ones responsible for the child's conversion. "We are to balance our zeal with confidence in a sovereign God. Faith comes by hearing and hearing by the Word of God" (Romans 10:17).[82]

Too often, an appeal to accept Christ can be pushed upon children.

One needs to remember that the Gospel, when appropriately and clearly presented, has its own appeal, and the work of the Holy Spirit has its own power (161). When offering an invitation or asking for a child's response, one should:

- Ask children to respond "inside" as opposed to an outward response. One might say to the children, "If you want Jesus to be your Savior, say to Him, 'Yes, Jesus, I want You to be my Savior.'" Avoid group decisions. If possible, have volunteers trained to counsel, so when you have a group of children ready to talk about salvation, you too are ready.
- Encourage children to talk with you or their parents if they want Jesus to be their Savior. When they come, ask them why they want to talk. Should a child say, "Can I accept the Lord or ask Jesus to be my Savior?" then that is an opportunity that should not be put off.
- Be mindful of statements like "ask Jesus into your heart" and other simplistic phrases that may lead to a decision that is not genuine or not even meaningful. For young children, the phrase "ask Jesus into your heart," when taken literally, is a scary proposition and can be a detriment rather than an encouragement. Older elementary children have more of an understanding that something will not literally cut through their flesh and blood to reach their physical heart. However, if you do not know the children you are teaching well, use phrases such as "choosing to follow Jesus" or "asking Jesus to be my leader or boss."

Confession should be part of a child's response to the Gospel. Children often find it difficult to admit they are sinners or have disobeyed God. When under the conviction of the Holy Spirit, they should be able to voice that they have sinned.

- They need not confess a specific sin to you but should be encouraged to tell God and ask for His forgiveness as part of their response to the Gospel.

Childhood transgressions within the classroom are teachable moments in that they provide opportunities to speak to the heart of the child. Some of these opportunities include lying, stealing, disobeying parents, jealousy, and causing pain through unkind words and actions toward other children.[83] Discuss inappropriate behaviors with the child. Ask whether he or she has made a good choice or a bad one. Following the response, ask the child why the inappropriate behavior was a bad choice. Follow that with gently thinking through what might have been a better choice.

Be sensitive to the times when there is a heart response from the child and when the conversation may have opened the door for Gospel truths. Make every effort to resolve a child's guilt through admission of their wrong behavior to both you and, hopefully, God. Assure them that you have forgiven them and remind them that when we ask God, He will forgive, as well.

Shortly after completing a chapter on this topic within *Distinctively Christian: A Christ-centered Approach to Early Childhood Spiritual Development*, I (Milt) read an online post from a former student at Columbia International University. Caleb was following his calling as a third-grade Christian schoolteacher and is now serving as a youth minister in Milpitas, CA. I believe his reflection provides the perfect conclusion for this chapter.

> *Today in class, I felt led to share the Gospel for the 15th time (or more) this year and give an invitation. Two of my students decided to follow Jesus...that makes five in all this year. So many teachers are ready for the end of the school year and counting down the days. It's easy to give up at the end, but I'm kind of sad and trying to treasure every last minute I have with these kids.*
>
> *I've grown to love them so much, and many days, I feel like I have the best profession in the world. I get to disciple kids and teach them about Jesus. I don't think you can find anything better to do with your time than that! "Be always abounding in the work of the Lord, knowing that in the Lord your labour is not in vain." 1 Cor. 15:58*
>
> Caleb Hankin, Freedom Christian Academy, Fayetteville, NC
> Now serving as a youth minister in Milpitas, CA

Reflect and Respond

1. Consider the Bible curriculum you currently use. To what degree does it provide the foundation for the Big Story? Are the individual stories sequential and held together under the theme of God's love (grace), promises, and plan?

2. Think through the Gospel narrative that you share with children. Is the language or story in alignment with the language presented by your Bible curriculum? Is it culturally responsive?

3. What is your response when there are authentic opportunities to invite students to believe and follow Jesus?

4. John Piper, in a message to his congregation, said, "Be like children in relation to God and be like God in relation to children." [84] Explain your interpretation of this quote based upon your reading and understanding of this chapter.

Part Two

Developing Focus Through
an Elementary Ministry's
Missional Framework

Chapter Eight

Developing a Mission, Vision, and Desired Outcomes for an Elementary-Level Ministry

Him, we **proclaim, warning everyone and teaching** everyone with all wisdom that we may present everyone **complete in Christ**.

Colossians 1:28

My goal is that they may **be encouraged in heart and united in love** so that they may have the full riches of **complete understanding**, in order that they may **know the mystery of God, namely, Christ.**

Colossians 2:2

Let love be genuine. Abhor what is evil, hold fast to what is good. Love one another with brotherly affection. Outdo one another in showing honor. Do not be slothful in zeal, be fervent in spirit, serve the Lord. Rejoice in hope, be patient in tribulation, be constant in prayer. Contribute to the needs of the saints and seek to show hospitality.

Romans 12:9-13

The Apostle Paul was a missional thinker. Throughout the Epistles, the content of his writing and teaching was a reflection of his purpose, mission, vision, and desired outcomes. A fruitful children's ministry must, likewise, be mission-driven and made explicit through a curriculum framework if the vision is to become a reality. The mission and vision are the starting point for a program's curriculum because when instruction begins with the end in mind, we define and clarify the program's desired outcomes.

Many mission statements are actually purpose statements or statements of what the program proposes to do. The mission, however, is the "billboard" that portrays the distinctives of its product or what a child at the end (prior to moving to the middle school ministry or Sunday school) will know, be able to do, value, and believe. In other words, it provides a focus that keeps everything on track—a track that leads to the accomplishment of its mission.

Too often, an elementary program either has no mission or vision of its own or, when viewed within the context of student ministries as a whole (birth through high school), only identifies with the broader mission. The problem with the latter is that there is no focus on specific elementary-level outcomes to guide its practices and validate the effectiveness of its efforts. An upper elementary framework, because it is age-specific, strives to establish a biblical worldview, faith in Jesus, and growth as a young disciple that is age-appropriate or aligns with their level of cognitive and spiritual maturity.

Since the ministry framework's purpose, mission, and vision are often found online and in other published materials within the church, the realization of the end result is directly related to the integrity of the program. Families are trusting the children's ministry of their church to not only engage in its purpose but also accomplish its mission. All content and instructional activities within the classroom can and should be consistently linked to its intended outcomes. This safeguards against every teacher "doing and striving for what is right in their own eyes."

The labels for each part of a framework are secondary to their function; therefore, attention should be given to content as opposed to a label. In the end, it is the content, regardless of its label, that is critical.[85]

The Church
Go therefore and make disciples of all the nations, baptizing them in the name of the Father and the Son and the Holy Spirit, teaching them to observe all that I commanded you... Matthew 28:19-20a.

Local Congregation

Purpose, Mission, and Vision

Student Ministries

Purpose, Mission, and Vision

Upper Elementary Ministry

Purpose, Mission, Vision

and

Desired Outcomes

The Curriculum

The Assessment Plan

The Purpose

Many programs do not have a purpose statement separate from a mission statement. In fact, many view the two as being synonymous. However, a curriculum framework, as illustrated in the graphic, may include a purpose statement. A purpose statement, if included, **should clarify what the program does**. Paul's purpose, according to Colossians 1:20, was to proclaim, warn, and teach everyone with wisdom.

A purpose statement contains phrases like:

- The program partners with parents…
- The Sunday school supports the home in its effort to "train up a child in the way he should go."
- Through a Christ-centered philosophy and biblical instruction, teachers strive to provide a successful first step in a child's Christian education.
- Teachers model Christ and create learning communities where children are nurtured and encouraged.
- Volunteers within the children's ministry create a sense of community within the church where children can learn, grow, and fellowship with one another.

These examples all have purpose in common. They state what classrooms will be like and what teachers will do.

What they fail to do is point out the end result of their efforts.

The following is an example of a *purpose statement*:

The elementary ministry supports the church, its parents, and the surrounding community by providing biblically-based learning experiences where children study God's Word within an atmosphere of love and age-appropriate activities.

In the past, there has often been the assumption that if one fulfilled a prescribed set of tasks, then the student would learn and grow spiritually. Even if or when this is true, without an idea of specific or intended outcomes, how is one to measure the effectiveness of the program or curriculum?

If you discover that your program has a purpose, as opposed to a mission, statement, refer to it as the purpose statement and develop a separate mission statement. What is the elementary program to accomplish prior to and in preparation for the middle school program? That expectation should be expressed as the elementary ministry's mission. Paul's mission was to present everyone complete in Christ and, as noted in Colossians 1:29, it was to this end that Paul invested all his energy.

The Mission

The mission makes the primary goals of the program clear. It provides categories or "files" wherein all outcomes can be organized. It drives and directs the curriculum and provides the criteria needed to verify whether or not the program is doing what it has set out to do.

The following example of a mission statement provides eight areas of focus.

> It is the mission of the upper elementary ministry to increase students' understanding of the knowledge, skills, and dispositions related to a biblical, Christ-centered worldview. Children (ages 8 through 11) will come to know Jesus, choose to follow (obey) Him, and begin to live a life characterized by love and service to others and God's Kingdom. The ministry also strives to develop a partnership with families that increases their involvement and supports each child's spiritual growth and development.[86]

Based upon this mission statement, everything the elementary ministry hopes to accomplish should fit within these eight "files":

- A greater understanding of biblical **knowledge and concepts**
- Age-appropriate Bible study and Christian life **skills (e.g., prayer, locating a verse)**
- Christ-centered biblical **values and attitudes** (dispositions)
- A biblical **view of self** (including one's needs and purpose)
- **Knowing God and Jesus**
- Knowing **God's Word as truth**
- **Obedience**
- **Parent involvement and training**

The mission provides an initial overview of what the program will strive to accomplish, but one does not yet understand what is meant by each of these categories.

- What is the foundational age-appropriate knowledge or concepts related to faith development?

- What Bible study and life skills are related to faith development?
- What are the values, beliefs, and attitudes that characterize a follower of Christ and a biblical worldview?
- How should a child biblically view themselves and their purpose?
- What does knowing God and Jesus look like or involve during the primary years?
- How should a third-fifth-grader view the Bible (God's Word)?
- What are the "who," "what," and "why" related to obedience?
- What does the Bible say about family? How should a family work according to the Bible if there is only one parent or it is a blended family?
- What is the content and means related to parent training?
- How should parents be involved and aid the spiritual development of their children?

The Vision

The vision is an amplified version of the mission and should provide the answers to the aforementioned questions. If one were to ask a group of children's ministry directors for the answers to these questions, one might, due to differing viewpoints, receive different answers. However, the answers from within a specific program should be consistent and well-defined since they form the basis for everything that is taught and experienced. The vision should fit the context, align with the church's vision, and be developmentally appropriate.

Think of the vision in terms of an address to teachers and perspective parents in which the eight files within our example are opened and more specifically defined. The vision forecasts the desired impact or expected results at the conclusion of the upper elementary program.

Creating a mission and vision

Begin by asking leadership and a focus group of ministry volunteers to think through what upper elementary students, prior to moving to the middle school ministry, should have learned and become. Review the expected outcomes of the early childhood level as the foundation upon which you will build and continue to disciple. Also, examine what others (authors and researchers) view as desired outcomes in keeping with the student's emerging ability to move beyond preoperational thinking, based upon experiences, to thinking that is more conceptual in nature. The elementary outcomes should also align with the upper elementary level of social, cognitive, moral, and faith development (see Appendix A).

Through study, discussion, reflection, and prayer, use the information to brainstorm and create a list of the outcomes that will describe your "mission accomplished." The list below, based upon a recent (not necessarily comprehensive) review of literature, serves as an example of a brainstorming session. Keep in mind that this list is unlikely to represent your church and its history, mission, cultural context, and, most importantly, students since these factors are not known to us. Your task at hand is to create a list that fits *your* elementary ministry and its participants.

Brainstormed Outcomes:

Students will come to know that:

- God is always present, and He cares for us.
- God is our Father; Jesus is God's Son; the Holy Spirit is our helper (the Trinity).
- God created the heavens and the Earth.
- God is all-powerful and knows all things.
- The Bible is God's book written by authors inspired or directed by the Holy Spirit.
- The Bible contains God's one redemptive story in four major acts—creation, fall, redemption, and restoration.
- The Bible is the basis upon which Christians answer worldview questions—reality, truth, value, the nature of humankind, and the future.
- Satan, the redemptive story's antagonist, is a fallen angel who rebelled against God.
- Satan tempts Christians in order to lead them away from Jesus.
- The Bible shows us how followers or disciples of Jesus should live.
- God's commandments, which tell us what is right and wrong, and indicators of Christian character are found in the Bible.
- All people are made in God's image and are unique and wonderfully made.
- All people are sinners and need a Savior because they have disobeyed God.

- When Jesus died on the cross, it was for all people. He experienced the punishment for mankind's sins, and He offers forgiveness as a free gift.
- Jesus has prepared a place in Heaven for those who have chosen to follow Him.
- Jesus is coming again.
- There is a biblical view of marriage, familial roles, and the purpose of family.

Brainstormed Bible and Life Skills:

Students are able to:

- "Process spiritual questions independently and in small groups."[87]
- Recite Bible verses and selected passages related to topics (salvation, God's love for them, resisting temptation, stewardship, etc.).
- Begin to recognize (discern or think critically) ideas that do and do not represent a biblical worldview.
- Categorize Scripture (history, wisdom literature, major and minor prophets, gospels, epistles, poetry, etc.).
- Categorize the "acts" within God's story (creation, fall, redemption, restoration).
- Share the Gospel with others.
- Discuss the meaning of baptism.
- Use a Bible dictionary and concordance.
- Locate a verse within the Bible.
- Locate places or events within the Bible on a map.
- Offer praise and worship.
- Pray.

Brainstormed Dispositional Outcomes: *(values, beliefs, attitudes)*

Students desire or choose to...

- Confess sins and ask Jesus to be their Savior.
- Identify with the death and resurrection of Jesus through baptism.
- Talk to God through prayer.
- Love Him, follow Him, and bring Him glory.
- "Begin to make their parents' and church's faith their own."[88]
- Choose to honor and obey God and parents.

- Worship God through spiritual disciplines, including song, prayer, and service.
- Attend to God's Word and share it with others.
- Love, respect, be thankful for, and serve others (other-directed as opposed to self-directed living).
- Look for ways to be involved in the church.
- Seek God's calling or purpose for their life.

Program teachers and volunteers desire or choose to...

- View parents as the greatest influencers of their children's spiritual development and choose to involve them as the primary spiritual influencers of children.

The list need not include every potential outcome but should capture the essence of what will become the mission's and vision's priorities. Once finished, look for redundancy and ideas that can be consolidated into a single statement. Also, eliminate ideas that are an aspect of a larger or overarching idea. For example, the vision might include knowing or choosing to practice developmentally appropriate spiritual disciplines, while prayer, worship, and time in God's Word might be subsets of the bigger goal—spiritual disciplines. Having identified the goals, you are ready to write a mission and vision. The mission is a concise statement that reduces your goals to major categories (or files) as previously discussed. Finally, with mission statement in hand, you will be ready to write a vision that amplifies the categories within the mission.

There can be additional instructional outcomes that extend beyond those within the vision, but those within the vision are the *primary public goals* and subject to assessment.

Example Vision Statement for an Elementary Ministry

By the time fifth-grade students graduate from the elementary children's ministry, students will know that God, the creator and sustainer of life, loves and cares for them and desires to communicate with them through prayer. They will gain a clearer understanding of the Trinity and acknowledge God's power over all things both in Heaven and on

Earth. They will understand that Jesus, God's Son, came to Earth to be a demonstration of the truth and fulfill the Father's redemptive plan through His death and resurrection. They will know that the Holy Spirit, the comforter and guide, dwells within those who choose Jesus and that it is the Spirit that enables them to live a life pleasing to God.

They will accept the Bible as true and absolutely reliable. They will look to and accept the Bible's answers to life's important questions related to reality, truth, values, and humankind's nature and purpose (worldview). The Bible's every word, spoken by the Holy Spirit to those who wrote it, contains the history of God's people, His redemptive story, and His instructions for living a Kingdom-minded, purposeful life. As needed, they will be able to utilize a concordance or Bible dictionary to locate information related to topics within their lessons or when reading the Bible.

They will understand their need for salvation and choose to accept Jesus as the only means of salvation. They will desire to grow spiritually through obedience and begin the shift from a self-centered mindset to one that is other-directed. This shift will be evident as they seek to serve, share, and cooperate with one another. They will begin to view themselves as individuals uniquely created by God with gifts and talents to be used for God's glory.

Parents will accept their role as the primary influencers of their children's spiritual formation and choose to support the upper elementary program through teaching, modeling, and participating in the ministry's training opportunities and other family activities.

The Outcomes (restatement of the vision in outcome format)

This phase of the framework development involves the translation of the vision's goals into more explicit outcome statements. The mission and vision are public statements, whereas outcomes are for program use only. Outcomes are used as the basis for curriculum development and assessment. Outcomes are sometimes also referred to as goals or standards. Methods for writing outcomes vary, but once a style is selected, it should be used consistently. The outcome statements should reflect a performance that can be used for assessment in that it provides an indicator of how the learning is to be demonstrated.

This sampling of outcomes is based on the previous example of a vision statement.

Children will:

- Identify four or more attributes of God. (knowledge)
- Provide an overview of the redemptive story as recorded in the Bible and include aspects of creation, fall, redemption, and restoration. (knowledge)
- Use a Bible dictionary and concordance to increase one's understanding of a topic within a Bible lesson. (skill)
- Recognize or discern a non-biblical worldview when heard, viewed, or read. (skill)
- Testify to having asked Jesus to be their Savior and affirm a willingness to follow Him. (disposition)
- Demonstrate love and care (an other-directed rather than a self-centered attitude) by offering to help others in need and share things God has provided. (disposition)

Teachers will:

- Acknowledge and choose to involve parents as the greatest influencers of their children's spiritual development.

Parents will choose to:

- Attend parent focus groups and other forms of parent education. (disposition)

See Appendix B for the complete list of outcomes drawn from the elementary ministry's vision (page 130).

Reflect and Respond

Use the content and process within this chapter to work through the following questions:

1. What elements of the framework are currently available within your program? What elements are needed?

2. Write down your program's mission and, if available, its purpose statement. If your program does not have a mission statement, jot down some phrases that might capture the essence of what you hope to accomplish within the upper elementary ministry. Combine your ideas to form a mission statement.

3. Examine your mission statement for the "files" found within it. List these categories and explain what is meant by each one. Try writing a paragraph that represents each of the phrases within your mission. Use these paragraphs as the basis for your vision.

4. Work through the vision statement and highlight (color code) and number phrases that indicate what students will know (red), be able to do (blue), and choose to believe and value (green). Convert these into the three types of outcomes— knowledge, skills, and dispositions. A vision should include outcomes from each category.

There should be a sense of urgency in that, once students reach the preteen years, when independence is increasingly asserted, the transfer of trust and faith to God becomes more difficult.

Chapter Nine

Designing the Curriculum and Means to Verify Its Effectiveness

With mission, vision, and outcomes in place, the platform for curriculum has been prepared. Curriculum is simply all that will be said and done as a means of realizing the outcomes. Curriculum is developed or evaluated through the process of examining each outcome to determine if the means to achieve it is available. A series of questions, like those listed below, should be answered to both clarify and guide in the process.

- What are the related Bible stories or biblical truths that would form the basis for the outcome?
- What other content-specific materials (e.g., books and visuals) will be needed to reach this goal?
- What instructional strategies will facilitate the learning?
- What firsthand experience (e.g., field trips, weekend retreats, service opportunities, classroom visitors, summer camps) should be included?
- How can classroom environment contribute to reaching this outcome?
- What training will volunteers, leaders, and parents need in order to reach this outcome?

The answers to these questions are the components of the curriculum and, when available and utilized, provide the means to accomplish the mission. The curriculum can be developed or reviewed through a table or matrix that includes each outcome and the necessary means.

Example of a curriculum matrix

The Outcome	Materials	Instructional Strategies	Experiences	Classroom Environment
Skill **Outcome: 1** Use a Bible dictionary to amplify one's understanding of a topic within their Bible lesson. (skill)	Access to Bible dictionaries within the classroom.	Instruct children on how to use the dictionary. Provide opportunities for students to collaborate and summarize their insights.	Include Bible research activities as a means of amplifying or reviewing a lesson. Have students keep a journal of their insights.	Establish a safe place where inquiry is welcomed. Shift from teacher talk to student talk and engagement.

The chapters within part one of this book presented the biblical content, instructional strategies, and the role and dispositions of ministry volunteers related to the spiritual formation of children. Taken together, the book itself is a curriculum to accomplish the mission that has motivated the *Distinctively Christian* series. The curriculum framework, however, is not complete until an assessment plan has been developed.

Assessment and Evaluation

Assessment and evaluation are often neglected in discussions related to children's ministry curriculum. Yet it is an important success factor in that it verifies the effectiveness of a curriculum's experiences, content, and instructional strategies. Assessment is the gathering of data, and evaluation is the use of that data as a means of deciding whether or not objectives have been met. Even though children are providing the data, it is the effectiveness of the curriculum that is being evaluated. Assessment strategies provide input to a "dashboard" that when interpreted (evaluation) indicates whether or not the program is on course and then, ideally, provides ministry leadership and volunteers with an opportunity to experience the joy that comes from knowing that children are coming to know the Father and beginning to walk in the truth (1 John 14a and 3 John 3:4).

Assessment: An Integral Part of Effective Teaching

Gathering information related to what students know, how they are thinking, and what they are applying is at the heart of teaching that results in learning and change. If this is true, we should expect to see evidence of this practice when "observing" Jesus, the Apostle Paul, and other disciples as they taught and interacted with one another in both the Gospels and during the founding of the church.

Biblical Examples of Assessment	
Questioning	There are over 300 examples of Jesus asking questions during His teaching and interactions with His disciples and others. Some questions were directly related to a desire to know an individual's understanding and relationship to Jesus: "But who do you say that I am?" (Matthew 16, Luke 9 and Mark 8) and "Do you love me?" (John 21:17). In Luke 10:25-28, the Pharisee asked what he should do to inherit eternal life. As Jesus often did, He responded with a question to establish both not only what the Pharisee knew but also His understanding: "What is written in the law?" (knowledge) and "How do you see it?" (understanding) The Apostle Paul, while in Ephesus, met some disciples. Paul asked them, "Did you receive the Holy Spirit when you believed?" Consider the insight gained when they responded, "We haven't even heard that there is a Holy Spirit" (Acts 19:1-2).

Observing both firsthand (observation) and through reports or feedback from others (anecdotal information)	Paul was a keen observer. His observations revealed both what his "students" had and had not yet learned. Information was based upon both direct observation and reports from others.
	For example, Paul received a report that teaching had not yet changed or set apart the new believers from that of their Corinthian neighbors (1 Cor. 1:10-11). This information provided Paul with input that they needed more teaching in the area of being of one mind. The content of 1 Corinthians was responsive to that need. Anecdotal information showed that his mission, "every man complete in Christ," had not yet been realized.
	Paul also received feedback that the Thessalonians were showing love to one another throughout Macedonia. He was able to encourage them and spur them on to love even more (1 Thessalonians 4:9).
	When Priscilla and Aguila *heard* Apollos's bold instruction regarding the way of the Lord, they "took him aside and *explained to him the way of God more accurately*" (emphasis added; Acts 18:24-26).

> **Criterion-Referenced Assessments**
> (evaluating the learning of students based upon a set of pre-specified qualities)
>
> Regardless of the means, assessment must be grounded in objective, predetermined criteria stemming from the content of instruction. For example, when teaching students about patience, one will be showing students the meaning of patience by teaching what a patient person does and does not do. The content within the instruction thus provides a listing of what to look for when observing children. Are the children demonstrating patience or impatience? If children are asked to tell us what God is like, then a list of characteristics used during instruction would form the criteria for evaluation. The criteria are the means of objectively identifying the presence or absence of a disposition or the student's understanding of a concept.
>
> Paul's teaching within the Epistles was filled with criterion. For example, Paul's teaching regarding presenting our bodies as a living sacrifice listed possible outcomes in Romans 12:9-21. His teaching on the "new self" in Colossians 3 includes a list of what characterizes the taking off of the old and putting on the new self, and in 1 Corinthians 13:4-7, Paul defines love.
>
> These serve as examples related to Paul's teaching. Your criteria will relate to your teaching, developmentally appropriate application points, and the expectation of the Spirit's work within the child.

Creating an Assessment Plan:

Given a clearly defined objective, the means whereby the outcome will be verified is reflected by the verb within the outcome statement. The plan can be organized through a second matrix. This matrix will include the objective, the means whereby the student will demonstrate or make explicit his or her learning, the person who is responsible for performing the assessment, and the context or timing of the assessment.

Where appropriate, the method of measurement (converting data into numbers) should also be indicated in the matrix. The effectiveness of the curriculum, simply stated, is based upon the percentage of children who demonstrate the criteria needed to verify that the outcome has been reached.

Example of the assessment matrix:

The outcome	The student will	Who will assess	Context and timing	Measurement
Provide a broad overview of God's redemptive story. (knowledge)	Arrange in order a group of cards that represents, through pictures, symbols, or words, the various portions of the story and then use the "timeline" to verbally share the story.	The student's teacher or other volunteer with whom the student has been acquainted during their fifth-grade year.	The assessment will be done during a one-on-one interview with a familiar teacher or ministry volunteer.	Performance is measured based upon the accuracy of the timeline and an appropriate telling of the story. Data will be recorded by using a checklist of key elements or a rubric that describes criteria needed to demonstrate a performance level (mastery, satisfactory, needs improvement, and not met). Determine the percentage of students who meet the criteria at a satisfactory or mastery level as the benchmark to determine program success (e.g., 80% of the group should meet the criteria at or above the satisfactory level).
See Appendix F for additional examples of assessment strategies based upon the outcomes within Appendix B.				

Working through the Process

Developing an assessment plan can be created by answering a series of questions related to each framework objective. The discussion and example that follows will be based upon skill objective three within the sample framework (Appendix B).

The Design Process	
What is the outcome?	Framework objective (skill 3): Develop a means of explaining or sharing the Gospel
What type of assessment will be used? • Interview/ Questioning • Observations • Demonstration with criterion-based rubric • Parent questionnaire • Anecdotal record • Student journals and self-evaluation	A one-on-one interview in which the student is asked to explain the Gospel, either by memory or with the use of a familiar visual aid (e.g., wordless book).
What is the justification for using this method?	Throughout the program, the children have observed and listened to an oral presentation of the Gospel using a good news bracelet, wordless book, or other visual representation/memory aid. They have roleplayed sharing the Gospel with one another.
What are the criteria or indicators of success?	A logical or orderly outline of the Gospel that includes some of the vocabulary that has been modeled by the teacher and practiced by the students through interactive discussions during classroom activities.

How will the information be recorded or measured?	The teacher or familiar volunteer will use a checklist with the Gospel vocabulary and a five- or six-point outline of the Gospel. As the student shares his or her explanation of the Gospel, the vocabulary used during the explanation is checked off by the teacher (Love, sin, punishment, death, confess, repent, Jesus, God's son, died, blood, payment, sacrifice, forgiveness, new or eternal life, etc.). The major elements of the Gospel are likewise checked off with a notation as to whether or not the order was meaningful. The elements should align with the Gospel narrative (vocabulary) that is used throughout the program.
What will be the benchmark that determines whether or not the objective has been met?	The inclusion of all the words on the checklist would not be expected, but if the list has 15 or more words, 8-10 words might be a reasonable expectation. The required number is decided by ministry leadership. So, the "objective met" target for a student might be 8-10 words with at least one idea from within each part (e.g., pages in the wordless book) of the Gospel. The framework benchmark might be that at least 85% of the children who have participated in the ministry for two or more years will have met the objective. Note: This assessment measures knowledge of the Gospel as opposed to conversion or acceptance of the Gospel. The ministry teaches the truth, but the Holy Spirit completes the work.

How will this data be used?

The purpose of the assessment plan and the resulting data is to validate the effectiveness of the program or the degree to which the ministry is having an impact on the knowledge, skills, and dispositions related to a child's spiritual growth. If the objectives are important, and if valid means (curriculum) have been chosen and utilized, then objectives should be met at a satisfactory or mastery level. However, what happens if an objective is not met? One must then ask why. Have the methods and curriculum actually been used? If not, why not? If they have been used, then the curriculum related to the objective must be examined and either revised or replaced.

If the instructional methods appear to be well-chosen and utilized, then perhaps there might be other circumstances that are the cause. For example, in any given year, you may be evaluating a group of children where a noticeable number of students have struggled (for reasons outside the ministry's control) throughout their years within the program. If this is the case, then deciding to change curriculum based upon this group's performance may be a mistake. Program directors should note the unrealized objective but base a change on a repeated shortfall rather than on what might be an isolated occurrence. Appendix F presents additional examples of assessments based upon the outcomes within Appendix B.

Appropriate Practices

- Evaluations must align with teaching. All assessments must be preceded by instruction that is related to the knowledge, skill, belief, or attitude that will be assessed.
- The means by which an objective is assessed must be familiar to the student. If, for example, a child is to be interviewed, then the children should have had similar conversations with their teachers throughout the program.
- Informal or "formative assessments" should be ongoing throughout instruction. One should not wait until the end to determine if the students are moving toward mastery.
- Children should know and be comfortable with adults with whom they interact during the evaluation process.
- Children should not be told or sense that they are being evaluated. The children should be familiar with the activities used to gather information.
- *Do not use* data gathered from children unless they have participated for at least two years. Since you are evaluating the program, the data must represent children who have experienced the curriculum.
- If parents will be part of the assessment plan, it is important to build a relationship with them. Asking questions during informal conversations provides valuable information. Keep in mind that parents know their children, and their insights within the home are extremely valuable. When something noteworthy is shared, be sure and make note of it. This type of information

(referred to as an anecdotal record), though not planned, is useful in making decisions regarding program effectiveness.

- Data collected during the first year of the assessment plan should be considered a pilot assessment. The assessments need to be utilized to see if it is an effective means of gathering the data, along with evidence that the criteria and scoring method not only work but are a valid or true measure of the outcome.

Living the Curriculum Framework

A curriculum framework, and the work involved in creating it, is not designed to collect dust on an office shelf. It is designed as a program's roadmap to "mission accomplished" and should be referred to when training teachers, choosing curriculum, and designing lessons.

- Share the mission and vision with the public. It should be presented via a link to the children's ministry on the church's website and referred to when answering parent questions.
- Provide the entire framework to volunteer teachers as part of their orientation. Review the outcomes and point out how the curriculum is designed to fulfill the mission and its vision.
- Stay focused and follow the framework's plan.
- Utilize the assessment plan with fifth graders during the spring and summer months prior to promotion to the middle school program. It is applied in fifth grade because prior to this time the curriculum (means) has not yet been fully applied.
- Annually analyze the assessment data to evaluate the effectiveness of the curriculum. If an objective falls short of expectations, consider instructional changes that might result in more children reaching the goal. Be sure to evaluate whether all the components within the curriculum matrix are in place and being utilized or if perhaps a change of plan (the means) is needed.
- Consider the possibility that the vision may need revision due, for example, to inappropriate expectations for upper elementary students. Justify all changes without losing sight of the mission.
- Tie strategic planning and annual budgeting to changes that require funding.
- Provide an annual volunteer "state of the vision" address and a celebration of the met objectives.

Reflect and Respond

1. If you have been using a published curriculum and plan to keep using it, understand that your curriculum is actually based upon the publisher's mission and vision. Examine the curriculum to determine the publisher's purpose, mission, and vision. Does it align with yours? Do you need to supplement the curriculum to address all of **your desired outcomes**? Have you been assessing the effectiveness of this curriculum?

2. This chapter has discussed the means whereby a curriculum can be either evaluated or created. Select two of your desired outcomes and create a curriculum matrix for each one.

3. Develop an assessment matrix for the two outcomes used in question two.

4. If you are using a published curriculum, evaluate it for its alignment with your outcomes by using the curriculum to fill in the elements within each column of the matrix. This exercise can be used with all of your desired outcomes to determine whether you have the curriculum that will enable you to accomplish your mission. What can you do to fill in gaps or supplement the instruction within your present curriculum? Is it time to seek a new and better-aligned curriculum?

Afterword

Finishing the Loop

In the same way, faith by itself, if it is not accompanied by action, is dead.

James 2:17 (NIV)

"The great theologian John Calvin wrote, 'It is faith alone that justifies, but faith that justifies can never be alone.' The word 'alone' in James 2:17 simply means 'by itself.' True saving faith can never be by itself; it always brings life, and life produces good works."

Warren W. Wiersbe[89]

The church and its leadership, volunteers, and parents should know whether or not the church's children's ministry is accomplishing what it has been designed to do. Sadly, too often, the answer is unknown. George Barna found that many parents show little interest in spiritual growth. He found that leaders of children's ministries share Barna's belief, as exemplified by this comment by a ministry leader with 27 years of experience.

> I have never once had a parent come up to me and ask how their child is progressing spiritually. Every weekend, I get parent after parent chasing me down to ask about their kids. But what they want to know is whether or not their child showed up to class, whether their child

had his or her Bible, and whether their child was well behaved during the class. Nobody seems to care very much about how the child is doing spiritually, as if merely showing up two or three times a month precludes having to even ask the question.[90]

Barna ended his book, *Transforming Children into Spiritual Champions,* with the need for evaluation and this challenge:

> If we are serious about preparing our children to become spiritual champions—not just church members or Bible owners but individuals who live every moment of their lives for the cause of Christ and with a determination to be holy because God is holy—then we must incorporate some degree of assessment into the spiritual development processes that we introduce into kids' lives.[91]

Accomplishing something more has been the goal of this book. As outlined in chapter eight, it starts by identifying a vision for the spiritual development of children. Without defined goals, the question of why minister remains unclear. A program's curriculum framework answers "why" and sets forth a reason and motivation to recruit and sustain its volunteers. Once outcomes are aligned with instructional means (chapter nine), measuring whether or not each outcome has been reached provides not only an opportunity to encourage one another with a deserved "well done," but as areas of weakness are uncovered, the way to even greater effectiveness is clarified. Don't allow yourself to be satisfied with doing ministry, but rather look for the results of what is being done.

The appropriateness of assessing spiritual formation is questioned because it is related to matters of the heart, and these matters are viewed by many as difficult or even impossible to assess. Nevertheless, if teaching is directed to reach the heart, it is possible to examine the words and actions that proceed from the changed heart.

Even though only God can fully know the heart, ministry directors and teachers are nevertheless responsible for collecting data that will enable them to evaluate or judge the effectiveness of the ministry's efforts.

If assessing students seems a bit overwhelming, consider the fact that you are already using assessment strategies within your instruction. You ask students to recite or write their memory verse, you use questions at the beginning of a lesson to access prior knowledge or review the previous lesson, you observe student participation and behaviors, and you have informal conversations with parents. Start with what you are already doing and shift attention to the program's vision and look for evidence that aspects of the bigger picture are becoming a reality—journal your observations, and you will be well on your way to "closing the loop."

As you worked through the "Reflect and Respond" questions at the end of each chapter, you have already been journaling and engaging in assessing and evaluating your program. Act upon what you have learned. What can you celebrate, and what can you do to even more effectively teach and reach the next generation?

In light of the urgency—

> *May you have power together with all the Lord's holy people to understand Christ's love. May you know how wide and long and high and deep it is. And may you know His love, even though it can't be known completely. Then, you will be filled with everything God has for you. God is able to do far more than we could ever ask for or imagine. He does everything by His power that is working in us. Give Him glory in the church and in Christ Jesus. Give Him glory through all time and for ever and ever. Amen.*
>
> Ephesians 3:18-21 (NIV)

Distinctively Christian

Christ-centered Professional Development
for Early Childhood and Elementary Educators

 Book One -
Early Childhood
Spiritual Development

 Book Four -
Early Childhood
Ministry

 Book Two -
Early Childhood
Philosophy and
Principles

 Book Five -
Elementary Ministry

 Book Three -
Early Childhood
Teaching and
Learning

 Book Six -
The Biblical Plot

Learn more at www.DistinctivelyChristian.com
and www.WheatonPress.com

Appendix A

Elementary Developmental Stages: A Summary

Social Development: Erikson	Cognitive Development: Piaget	Moral Development: Kohlberg	Faith Development: Fowler
		All stages are included since students can "stall" at any point. **Stage: Obedience/ Punishment (Pre-Moral)** Age: Birth to 9 Characteristic: Moral or behavioral choices based upon the fear of a consequence (discipline). This reflects egocentrism, or egocentric thinking.	**Stage: Impressionistic (Intuitive)** Age: Primarily 2 to 7 (elementary students, however, continue to be impressionistic.) Characteristic: Faith is learned through the "rituals" or practices found within the community of faith. This is in keeping with the preoperational stage of thinking (Piaget) and the need for firsthand concrete experiences. Lessons should be reinforced through play, role play, and celebrations.

		Stage: Self-Interest	Stage: Mythic
		Age: Preschool (note, however, that some never advance beyond this level of moral thinking.) Characteristic: During this stage, the moral choices are related to whether a positive consequence (reward) is perceived as likely.	Literal Age: School-age children It is during this period that the story or narrative of one's faith is learned. Bible stories need to be linked to the ONE Redemptive Story as basis for the Gospel.
Stage: Industry vs. Inferiority Age: 6 through 12 Characteristic: Highly dependent on school and other learning environments. Success feeds industry, while repeated failures lead to an "I can't" attitude. Be careful when asking children to read out loud unless you are sure they are able. Children believe they are "what they can do."	Stage: Concrete Operational Age: 7 to 11 Characteristic: Can learn through language but still dependent on concepts experienced through concrete representations in the past.	Stage: Conformity and Interpersonal Accord Age: School-age, pre-teen Characteristic: Motivated by wanting to have a "good boy" or "good girl" image. Responsive to the desire to be accepted or to fit in.	Stage: Conventional (conforming) Age: 12 to adulthood Characteristic: Faith is seen from the perspective of belonging to one's family, culture, or expectation. This aligns with what is sometimes referred to as "cultural Christians." It is centered on belonging as opposed to personal belief.

	Stage: Formal Operational	Stage: Authority and Social Order	Three **additional stages** follow, beginning in the mid-teens to adulthood. These stages begin as personal choice, individual (chosen) belief, and deepening levels of conviction. It is a rational belief based upon examination and personal choice. The highest level of faith is the willingness to stand alone, follow, and give one's life regardless of the consequences (selflessness). Considered a stage that is seldom reached.
	Age: 12 and up Characteristic: Now able to think about abstractions or ideas (concrete foundation still helpful but not always necessary).	Age: Pre-teen, teen Characteristic: A shift to acknowledging that there is a social order (external rules) that should be applied. Choices are responsive to laws and desires of society as opposed to personal gain.	
		Stage: Social Contract Age: Teens Characteristic: Right and wrong begin to be shaped by personal values with some legislated laws governing choices. By the end of this stage personal moral principles are more important than societal laws.	

Information regarding the stages of cognitive, social, moral, and faith development are easily accessible through online searches. Websites used in compiling the comparisons in Appendix A were retrieved April 2020:

http://www.psychologycharts.com/james-fowler-stages-of-faith.html

https://www.psychologynoteshq.com/kohlbergstheory/
https://www.verywellmind.com/piagets-stages-of-cognitive-development-2795457
https://courses.lumenlearning.com/teachereducationx92x1/chapter/
eriksons-stages-of-psychosocial-development/

Appendix B

Example of a Curriculum Framework: The Mission, Vision, and Outcomes for an Elementary Ministry

The Mission

It is the _mission_ of the Upper Elementary Level Ministry to increase the child's understanding of a biblical Christ-centered, worldview.

Children (ages 8-11) will:

1. Come to know Jesus,
2. Choose to follow Him, and
3. Begin to live a life characterized by love and service to others, the church, and God's Kingdom

The ministry also strives to develop a partnership with families that increases their involvement in ministry activities and supports their child's spiritual growth and development.

The vision (a more detailed, or amplified, description of the mission)

Upon completion of grade five, students will know that God, the creator and sustainer of life, loves and cares for them and desires to communicate with them through prayer. They will gain a clearer understanding of the Trinity—God as three persons—and acknowledge God's power over all things both in Heaven and on Earth. They will understand that Jesus, God's Son, came to Earth to be a demonstration of the truth and fulfill the Father's redemptive plan through His death and resurrection. They *will know that the Holy Spirit, the comforter and guide, dwells within those who choose Jesus and that it is the Spirit that enables them to live a life pleasing to God.*

They will accept the Bible as true and absolutely reliable. They will look to and accept the Bible's answers to life's important questions related to reality, truth, values, and humankind's nature and purpose (worldview). The Bible's every word, spoken by the Holy Spirit to those who wrote it, contains the history of God's people and His redemptive story and His instructions for living a Kingdom-minded, purposeful life. When needed, they will be able to utilize a concordance or Bible dictionary to locate information related to topics within their lessons or when reading the Bible.

They will understand their need for salvation and choose to accept Jesus as the only means of salvation. They will desire to grow spiritually through obedience and begin the shift from a self-centered mindset to one that is other-directed. This shift will be evident as they seek to serve, share and cooperate with one another. They will begin to view themselves as individuals uniquely created by God with gifts and talents to be used for His glory.

Ministry teachers, volunteers, and parents will work together to model, teach, and support one another. Parents will participate in ministry activities and communicate with teachers regarding a child's needs and spiritual growth.

The Outcomes: (restatement of the vision in outcome format)

This phase of the framework development involves the translation of the vision's implicit goals into a list of explicit outcome statements. The mission and vision are public statements, whereas outcomes are for program use only. Outcomes are used as the basis for curriculum development and assessment. Outcomes are sometimes also referred to as goals or standards. The outcome statements should reflect a performance that can be used for assessment in that it provides an indicator of how learning is to be demonstrated.

Knowledge

At the end of fifth grade, children will be able to:

1. Identify four or more attributes of God
2. Provide an overview of the redemptive story as recorded in the Bible (to include aspects of creation, fall, redemption, restoration)
3. Recognize Jesus as the second person within the Trinity and explain His role in God's plan for men, women, boys, and girls
4. Identify the role of the Holy Spirit in the life of the believer
5. Know how the Bible came into being and the Bible's relationship to truth
6. Answer the four basic questions within a biblical worldview
7. Know basic elements of a naturalist and humanist worldview

Skills

At the end of fifth grade, children will be able to:

1. Use a Bible dictionary and concordance to increase one's understanding of a topic within a Bible lesson.
2. Recognize or discern a non-biblical worldview when heard, viewed, or read
3. Develop a means of explaining or sharing the Gospel

Dispositions

At the end of fifth grade, children will be able to:

1. Testify to having asked Jesus to be their Savior and affirm a willingness to be discipled and follow Him
2. Recognize and value their uniqueness as one created by God
3. Demonstrate love and care (an other-directed rather than a self-centered attitude) by offering to help others in need and share things that God has provided
4. Choose to demonstrate gratitude, kindness, generosity, empathy, forgiveness, and love to others.[92]
5. Choose God's will and obedience over a desire to go one's own way
6. Value their talents and spiritual gifts and develop them as a means to glorify God
7. Seek God's calling or purpose for their lives

Parents will:

1. Support the learning of memory work and model biblical principles at home
2. Attend parent focus groups and other forms of parent education
3. Provide information on their child's spiritual growth during both informal and formal conferencing

Appendix C

Advent and Other Holiday Celebrations

What memories of Advent or Christmas do you have? If you are like me (Anne Marie), I remember live nativities, songs, and *lots* of candles. Each Sunday, my family would light an Advent wreath and read Scripture in anticipation of both Jesus' coming and coming again. Consequently, with my children, we have an Advent wreath, we light the candles, and we read Advent-related Scripture each week during Advent.

Holiday rituals matter. Be intentional with your time at home and church. Advent, the four weeks prior to Christmas, is a meaningful holiday tradition to incorporate into your family and church worship schedule. Advent begins on the fourth Sunday before Christmas and culminates on Christmas Day. Advent traditions can also be easily added to the Christmas curriculum within your church.

For Families:

For families with preschool children or younger, do not think that they will not "get" the idea of Advent. Little children understand the idea of waiting. They may not be "good at" waiting, but they understand the idea of not getting what you want right away. For elementary children, you can use the time of Advent for conversations related to God's promises, His faithfulness, Jesus' coming to Earth to dwell among us, His coming into the hearts of those who trust Him, and His coming again. It is a time of preparation, anticipation, and celebration.

Advent is a time of waiting and expectation. During the four weeks leading up to Christmas, discuss the idea of waiting. What emotions do they feel? (Excitement? Anxiousness? Longing? Frustration?) What examples, related to waiting, does your child or students have? (Waiting in a doctor's office? Waiting to take their turn? Waiting for mom to stop talking with a friend?)

To build on the ideas of expectation and waiting, create a countdown to Christmas Day. You can create a paper chain and take off a link each day as December 25 comes closer. Use a Jesse Tree and add the ornament for each day. Consider adding pieces to a nativity scene, with baby Jesus being placed in the scene on Christmas morning. You can use a store-bought Advent calendar with pieces of chocolate. Whatever you choose, be sure to talk to your children about the Christmas story throughout the month. Emphasize that even as the people awaited the first coming of their Messiah (our Savior), we too await the celebration of His coming again.

For Churches:

Many liturgical churches automatically celebrate Advent within their church calendars. If your church does not, then you can easily add it to your curriculum. In your schedule, set aside the four Sundays before Christmas Day. I recommend getting a wreath, or at least the candles (three purple, one pink, and one white).

What truths related to Christmas will you be teaching during the four weeks? If not already in your curriculum, you have plenty to choose from. You could cover the Old Testament prophecy of the Messiah, Zechariah and Elizabeth, the annunciation, Joseph's dream, Jesus' birth, and/or the shepherds.

Each Sunday, as you teach the group, light the appropriate candles for the week. You will also want to explain the candle and why it is a certain color. Most of the time, the candles represent hope, love, joy (pink), and peace, with the white candle being the Christ candle. Other churches might choose to have the first candle be the prophecy candle, the second is the Bethlehem candle, the third (pink) is the shepherd's candle, and the fourth is the angel's candle. Be creative and make up a theme for each year.

Because children learn through experiences and repetition, use the Advent wreath during the Bible study hour. Also choose a family to light the candle during the worship service and lead the congregation in a short Scripture reading, devotion, or prayer. This will allow children to have an opportunity to be a part of the larger community of believers. Parents can allow their children to participate in leading worship by reading Scripture, leading the prayer, or lighting the candle.

One teaching tip: Please do not include the traveling magi with your Christmas story plans. Scripture is clear that they were not at the manger and arrived later, after the birth of Jesus. If you want to teach the magi, wait until January. The first Sunday in January, or January 6 if celebrating at home, is Epiphany (the twelfth day of Christmas). This day on the church calendar celebrates the coming of the magi and, more importantly, that Jesus came not just to the Jews, but also Gentiles—every nation.

Devotional Resources for Advent Celebrations:

- *A Way to the Manger: A Family Advent Devotional* by Jeff Land
- *God With Us: A Family Advent Celebration* by Catherine Pawlak
- *Unwrapping the Greatest Gift: A Family Celebration of Christmas* by Ann Voskamp
- *The Advent Storybook: 25 Bible Stories Showing Why Jesus Came* by Laura Richie
- *The Shepherd on a Search: A 25 Day Family Devotional* by Josh Helms
- *Christ-Centered Advent: Family Devotions Based on Christmas Carols* by Hal and Melanie Young
- *Advent Book Series* by Arnold Ytreeide (Perfect for upper elementary and up!)
- *How to Make a Jesse Tree and Daily Readings:* http://www.crivoice.org/jesse.html
- *Prepare Him Room* curriculum package by Marty Machowsky

A Holiday "Curriculum"

The Celebration	Theme	Biblical References
These celebrations are offered as examples and options. Programs should feel free to add or delete based on developmental appropriateness, school calendar, curriculum alignment, and other cultures, etc.	Romans 14:5-8: Regardless of the celebration, celebrate as unto the Lord and for His glory.	Not intended for Bible memory but as the basis for the themes.
Labor Day	The importance of calling (designed for a special work) and glorifying God through our work	2 Timothy: 1: 8b -9 Colossians 1:28-29
Grandparents Day (Celebrated at different times around the world)	Respect for elders and their love and wisdom	Proverbs: 4: 20-22
Halloween	The evening before the church "turned" from darkness into light, declaring the truth in a culture that does not know it	Acts 26:16-18
Thanksgiving	In all things, give thanks.	Psalm 100: 4-5
Christmas	From Heaven to a stable, for you and me	Luke 2:1-20
New Year's Day Chinese New Year is celebrated according to lunar calendar.	God's faithfulness over the past year and anticipating His presence in the new year	Psalm 89:1-2
Martin Luther King Jr.'s Birthday	All men are created equal yet unique.	Galatians 3:28 John 8:36 Acts 7:34

Valentine's Day	Abiding in and sharing God's great love	John 15:9-11

1 Corinthians 13 |
Washington's Birthday	The importance of God's Word as the foundation for a country	Deuteronomy 6:1-3
St. Patrick's Day	A focus on missions	Matthew 28:19-20
Pre-Easter, six weeks	Christ's ministry of love	Selected teaching and events: John 2-11
Easter	He lives.	John 20
Earth Day, April 22	Stewardship of God's creation	Genesis 1:28-30
Mother's Day	Honor mothers and their importance to the family	Ephesians 6:2
Memorial Day	Christ calls on Christians to lay down their lives for Him and for the freedoms we enjoy.	John 15:13
Flag Day	Respect for the country and its leaders	Romans 13:1-4
Father's Day	Honor fathers and their importance to the family	Matthew 19:19
National Independence Day celebrations	God has ordained and established nations and governments. Pray for our country and its leaders.	Romans 13

Special Note: Add state or national holidays, where appropriate, that are unique to your country or that represent the cultural diversity within your classroom.

Appendix D

Critical Thinking Through Children's Literature

This article by Milton Uecker was first published in Make Way for Books (MWFB),
a newsletter publication by Dr. Kevin D. and Julie Washburn

What is critical thinking? When teachers are asked this question, words like "reason, discern, analyze, understand, argue, defend, and evaluate" are typical responses. However, when it comes to critical thinking, Christian educators need to move beyond definitions to a conviction that critical and higher-level thinking skills are appropriate for application within Christian education.

Critical thinking is often mentioned in the Bible. Paul, for example, described his role as **defender** of the Gospel. His habit was to **reason** in the synagogue (Acts 17) and he prayed that his students would be filled with spiritual **wisdom and understanding** (Colossians 1:9). He also prayed for the **depth of insight** that would be the foundation for discernment (Philippians 1:9-10). There is a relationship between higher-level thinking and critical thinking but there is an important distinction between the two. Critical thinking is one of the levels within the scope of higher-level thinking. Critical thinking is always focused on evaluation or judgment. It involves knowledge, understanding, and analysis as the basis for judgment, but critical thinking occurs when one applies thinking to criticize, defend, appraise or grade concepts and ideas. It is the ability to judge and defend that directly relates to worldview thinking.

All thinking proceeds from an individual's worldview or set of beliefs (philosophy). In his book, *Worldviews in Conflict*, Ronald Nash defines worldview as a "comprehensive, systematic view of life and of the world as a whole." He goes on to state that "no believer can be really effective in the arena of ideas until he or she has been **trained**

to think in worldview terms" (14). Elementary students, based upon their emerging understanding of worldview, are becoming increasingly aware of competing worldviews in movies and TV programs as well as the books and textbooks they read and study. Scripture describes these ideas as founded upon human tradition and thus hollow and deceptive (Colossians 2:8). Critical thinking equips them to recognize these deceptions and react rather than absorb. In reality, many faulty ideas have already impacted their young minds. It is because of this that Christian thinkers and teachers must guide students through the process of mind renewal (Romans 12:2).

Since everyone thinks from a philosophy, it follows that every author, including the writers of children's literature and movies, writes from the presuppositions of a worldview. Literature, whether read to or by children, can therefore be used to practice the analysis and discernment skills that characterize critical thinking. Children are regularly introduced to the thinking of other worldviews, whether or not we choose to acknowledge it. We can, however, influence whether or not children evaluate the author's ideas and values by discerning whether the idea aligns with God's Word.

Discerning worldviews begins with a knowledge and understanding of the answers to the questions that a worldview addresses (found within chapters three through six of this book). Unless the students learn to recognize the truth, they cannot detect the counterfeit. During critical thinking discussions, students must compare what they are hearing or reading again the truth. They must also be able to defend their conclusions by referencing a reliable source or benchmark that justifies their opinion. As children are discipled and memorize Scripture (see Appendix E), they can defend their worldview with the response, "It is written."

Philosophy in and of itself requires higher-level thinking since it deals with many abstractions. Worldview analysis, therefore, is most effectively integrated into the middle school. There are, however, upper elementary students who are beginning to ask questions and recognize that what they are hearing and learning while at church is different from what is valued or believed within their culture at large. This is particularly true of books and movies that are aimed at their interests. When parents and teachers engage children in a discussion as to the correctness of ideas, they are "scaffolding" their students to new levels of thinking and understanding. As children mature, their thinking will become more specific and insightful, but even young children who have become drawn into a good story can play the "worldview detective" role and uncover clues as to a writer's worldview through the thoughts and behaviors of the characters they have created.

During read-aloud and book club discussions, students can be asked to listen or look for clues to see if something said or done within the story deals with a worldview question. When the answer is "yes," then they should be able to point out the position of the writer and justify their conclusion by showing the statement or event that was their cue. Finally, the student should identify and compare their clue with biblical truth. Once they can do this you know that they are becoming an engaged and discerning reader and thinker. They have provided evidence that they can listen carefully, detect and analyze worldview vocabulary, determine the worldview position, defend their decision, and provide a biblical defense—vision accomplished. Some may even be able to take it to the highest level of thinking, synthesis and creation, by writing a portion of the story as it might be written from the perspective of a Christ-centered viewpoint.

To reach this level of thinking, students must have teachers who have practiced worldview analysis and can then model these thinking skills. As parents and teachers read aloud, they too can "think aloud" by sharing their reaction to something that happened or was said within the story. During or at the conclusion of a chapter or book, ask:

- Do you think the author a Christian?
- From what worldview is the author writing?
- Can you read a statement that cued you into her worldview? What worldview question is being answered by this clue?
- How is this belief different from yours?
- What is the basis for this belief? For your belief?
- What kind of behaviors stem from this kind of thinking?
- What are the consequences of this belief or value?
- What would you say to someone who holds these beliefs?
- Can you think of another movie or story with a similar worldview?
- Can you think of a story that deals with this issue from a biblical perspective?
- How would a Christian character respond in this same situation?

As teachers, we strive to connect truth to life, playing the role of a worldview detective is one means to that end. Consider how far beyond the ability to merely recall a Bible story a student detective will have progressed. More importantly, consider the degree to which they have been discipled.

Where does one begin? Teachers should consider literature that has received a literary award. The Newbery Award for example is "awarded annually by the Association for Library Service to Children, a division of the American Library Association, to the author of the most distinguished contribution to American literature for children."[93] These books often reflect the "age" in which they were written. They deal with contemporary issues and values and so provide a window into not only the life of the characters within the books but also the culture surrounding the lives of your students.

An example: *Shiloh* by *Phyllis Reynolds Naylor*. Published by Atheneum in 1991 and winner of the Newbery Award.[94] Shiloh is a hunting dog that is being abused by its owner in the hills of West Virginia. The main character, 11-year-old Marty, is determined to use any and all means to save this dog from its owner. These means include stealing, lying, and blackmail.

At first glance, it may seem these behaviors would deem this book inappropriate for use within Christian schools and church ministries. However, these behaviors reflect the thinking of a man-centered relative value system where the end (rescuing a dog) justifies the means. The well-being of the dog becomes a value that supersedes the lesson this boy has learned about honesty from his parents and his church. My experience has shown when discussed within a Christian context, children are quick to identify the faulty thinking, and they easily detect the consequences, including a guilty conscience, that stems from his behavior. Students recognize that questions regarding a moral code and the nature of boys (and girls) are the worldview issue. It is also a book in which alternative behaviors (solutions to the problem) can be identified.

Leading worldview discussion must begin with planning and practice by the teacher. Always read the literature selections prior to selection in order to judge not only their appropriateness but also the degree to which worldview is explicit enough to be recognized by the students. I am not suggesting that all books and their content are up for grabs—you are the gatekeeper, and you are the one that must decide. You must, however, also move beyond the idea that a book that contains secular thinking is out of bounds, especially if and when the selection can be discussed with parents and other mentors. Book club gatherings are a great way to involve parents. Appendix G lists a sampling of books that might help you take the first step. For more insight into conducting a book club, I encourage you to read *Deconstructing Penguins* by Lawrence and Nancy Goldstone.

A Christian mind must be cultivated throughout a child's Christian education. Children must be prepared to "stand alone" through the acquisition of intellectual courage. Don't wait until you feel ready. You will learn and grow right along with the children. Consider these famous words from Nike, "Just Do It." If you wait until you feel ready, it may never happen.

Appendix E

Worldview Memory Verses

Reality (Metaphysics)

- *In the beginning God created the heavens and the Earth. (Genesis 1:1)*
- *God saw all that He had made, and it was very good. (Genesis 1:31a)*
- *All things were made through God, and without Him nothing was made. (John 1:3)*
- *For by Him all things were created that are in Heaven and that are on the Earth, the things that are visible and the things that are invisible. (Colossians 1:16)*
- *He gives to all life, breath, and all things...for in Him we live and move and have our being. (Acts 17:28)*
- *The Earth is the Lord's and all it contains. (Psalm 103:19)*
- *But our God is in Heaven. He does whatever He pleases. (Psalm 115:3)*
- *(God said) For I am God, and there is no other; I am God, and there is no one like Me. (Isaiah 46:9)*
- *God is light and in Him there is no darkness at all. (John 1:5)*
- *The eternal God is your refuge (safe place). (Deuteronomy 33:27)*
- *The one who does not love does not know God because God is love. (1 John 4:8)*
- *Holy, holy, holy is the Lord God Almighty, who was and is and is to come. (Revelation 4:8b)*
- *You shall have no other Gods before me. (Exodus 20:3)*
- *But the Lord is the true God; He is the living God, the eternal King. When He is angry, the earth trembles; the nations cannot endure His wrath. (Jeremiah 10:10)*
- *God is not a man, that He should lie, nor a son of man, that He should change His mind. Does He speak and then not act? Does He promise and not fulfill? (Numbers 23:19)*

- *But God made the Earth by His power; He founded the world by His wisdom and stretched out the heavens by His understanding. (Jeremiah 10:12)*
- *But the Lord, who brought you up out of Egypt with mighty power and outstretched arm, is the One you must worship. To Him you shall bow down and to Him offer sacrifices. (2 Kings 17:36)*
- *Yours, O Lord, is the greatness and the power and the glory and the majesty and the splendor, for everything in Heaven and Earth is Yours. Yours, O Lord, is the kingdom; You are exalted as head over all. (1 Chronicles 29:11)*
- *Nothing in all creation is hidden from God's sight. Everything is uncovered and laid bare before the eyes of Him to whom we must give account. (Hebrews 4:13)*
- *Great is our Lord and mighty in power; His understanding has no limit. (Psalm 147:5)*
- *Hear, O Israel: The Lord our God, the Lord is one. (Deuteronomy 6:4)*

Verses related to God and His nature[95]:

- God is eternal: Psalm 90:1-2
- God is infinite in His presence: Psalm 139:7-8
- God is holy: Leviticus 19:2 and Revelation 4:8
- God is just: Ezekiel 18:25-29, Romans 2:9-11
- God is loving: Lamentations 3:22-2, 1 John 4:7-11

Desiring God Ministries has developed a resource to teach God's attributes to children. An attribute for each letter of the alphabet is presented as a series of lessons.[96]

Truth (Epistemology)

- *Sanctify them through Thy truth; Thy word is truth. (John 17:17)*
- *"This God—His way is perfect; the word of the Lord proves true... (Psalm 18:30a ESV)*
- *But he said, "Blessed rather are those who hear the Word of God and keep it." (Luke 11:28 ESV)*
- *Jesus said.... "I am the way, and the truth, and the life. No one comes to the Father except through me." (John 16:13 ESV)*

- *"…. your word is truth, and every one of your righteous rules lasts forever." (Psalm 119:160 ESV)*
- *Jesus said, "Heaven and Earth will pass away but my words will not pass away." (Mark 13:31 ESV)*
- *Jesus said, "If you stay in my word, you are truly my disciples, and you will know the truth…" (John 8:31 ESV)*
- *You are near, oh Lord, and all your commandments are the truth. (Psalm 119:151 ESV)*
- *"Everyone then who hears these words of mine and does them will be like a wise man who built his house on the rock." (Matthew 7:24 ESV)*
- *For everything that was written in the past was written to teach us, so that through endurance and encouragement of the Scriptures we might have hope. (Romans 15:4)*
- *Now all has been heard; here is the conclusion of the matter: Fear God and keep His commandments, for this is the duty of all mankind. (Ecclesiastes 12:13)*
- *I will raise up for them a prophet like you from among their brothers; I will put My words in His mouth, and He will tell them everything I command Him. If anyone does not listen to My words that the prophet speaks in My name, I Myself will call him to account. (Deuteronomy 18:18-19)*
- *For what I received I passed on to you as of first importance: that Christ died for our sins according to the Scriptures. That He was buried, that He was raised on the third day according to the Scriptures. (1 Corinthians 15:3-4)*
- *Jesus did many other miraculous signs in the presence of His disciples, which are not recorded in this book. But these are written that you may believe that Jesus is the Christ, the Son of God, and that by believing you may have life in His name. (John 20:30-31)*
- *When the Gentiles heard this, they were glad and honored the word of the Lord; and all who were appointed for eternal life believed. The word of the Lord spread through the whole region. (Acts 13:48-49)*
- *So then, brothers, stand firm and hold to the teachings we passed on to you, whether by word of mouth or by letter. (2 Thessalonians 2:15)*
- *I have no greater joy than to hear that my children are walking in the truth. (3 John 4)*

- *Blessed is the one who reads the words of this prophecy, and blessed are those who hear it and take to heart what is written in it because the time is near. (Revelation 1:3)*
- *Blessed are they who keep His statutes and seek Him with all their heart. (Psalm 119:2)*
- *No prophecy of Scripture comes from someone's own interpretation, For no prophecy was ever produced by the will of man, but men spoke from God as they were carried along by the Holy Spirit. (2 Peter1: 20-21)*
- *All Scripture is breathed out by God and profitable for teaching, for reproof, for correction, and for training in righteousness, that the man of God may be competent, equipped for every good work. (2 Timothy 3:16-17)*

Value (Axiology)

- *(Jesus said) "You shall love your God with all your heart, with all your soul, and with all your mind. This is the first great commandment" (Matthew 22:36a).*
- *...and the second is this. You shall love your neighbor as yourself" (Matthew 22:36b).*
- *...What does the Lord your God require (expect) of you, but to fear the Lord your God, to walk in all His ways" (Deuteronomy 10:12).*
- *(Jesus said)"...if you want to enter into life, keep the commandments" (Matthew 19:17).*
- *"...the one who does the will of God lives forever" (1 John 2:17b).*
- *"...now abides faith, hope, and love, but the greatest of these is love" (1 Corinthians 13:13).*
- *Don't use bad language. Say only what is good and helpful to those you are talking to and what will give them a blessing" (Ephesians 4:29).*
- *"But seek first His kingdom and His righteousness, and all these things will be added to you" (Matthew 6:33).*
- *"Fix your thoughts on what is true and good and right. Think about things that are pure and lovely and dwell on the fine, good things in others" (Philippians 4:8).*
- *"...put on a heart of compassion, kindness, humility, gentleness, and patience..." (Colossians 3: 12).*

- *And without faith it is impossible to please God because anyone who comes to Him must believe that He exists and that He rewards those who earnestly seek Him. (Hebrews 11:6)*
- *Let us fix our eyes on Jesus, the author and perfector of our faith, who for the joy set before Him endured the cross, scorning its shame, and sat down at the right hand of the throne of God. (Hebrews 12:2)*
- *This is the confidence we have in approaching God; that if we ask anything according to His will, He hears us. (1 John 5:14)*
- *And pray in the Spirit on all occasions with all kinds of prayers and requests. With this in mind, be alert and always keep on praying for all the saints. (Ephesians 6:18)*
- *A new command I give you: Love one another. As I have loved you, so you must love one another. By this, all men will know that you are My disciples, if you love one another. (John 13:34-35)*
- *As a prisoner for the Lord, then, I urge you to live a life worthy of the calling you have received. Be completely humble and gentle; be patient, bearing with one another in love. (Ephesians 4:1-2)*
- *Do nothing out of selfish ambition or vain conceit, but in humility consider others better than yourselves. Each of you should look not only to your own interests but also to the interests of others. (Philippians 2:3-4)*
- *And the Lord's servant must not quarrel; instead, he must be kind to everyone, able to teach, not resentful. Those who oppose him he must gently instruct, in the hope that God will grant them repentance leading them to a knowledge of the truth. (2 Timothy 2:24-25)*
- *And let us consider how we may spur one another on toward love and good deeds. Let us not give up meeting together, as some are in the habit of doing, but let us encourage one another – and all the more as you see the Day approaching. (Hebrews 10:24-25)*
- *Live in peace with each other. And we urge you, brothers, warn those who are idle, encourage the timid, help the weak, be patient with everyone. 1 (Thessalonians 5:13b-14)*
- *Be devoted to one another in brotherly love. Honor one another above yourselves. (Romans 12:10)*
- *Share with God's people who are in need. Practice hospitality. (Romans 12:13)*
- *In the same way, let your light shine before men, that they may see your good deeds and praise your Father in Heaven. (Matthew 5:16)*

- *Preach the Word; be prepared in season and out of season; correct, rebuke and encourage – with great patience and careful instruction. (2 Timothy 4:2)*
- *In everything set them an example by doing what is good. In your teaching show integrity, seriousness, and soundness of speech that cannot be condemned, so that those who oppose you may be ashamed because they have nothing bad to say about us. (Titus 2:7-8)*

Some longer passages:

- The Ten Commandments
- "The Marks of the True Christian," Romans 12:9-18
- "Put on the New Self," Colossians 3:12-17
- "The Fruit of the Spirit," Galatians 5:22-25

Humankind (Anthropology)

- ... *"So, God created man in His own image, in the image of God He created him; male and female He created them" (Genesis 1:27).*
- *"For we are His workmanship, created in Christ Jesus for good works" (Ephesians 2:10a).*
- *"I praise you for I am fearfully and wonderfully made. Wonderful are your works" (Psalm 139:14).*
- *"Fear God and keep His commandments, for this is the whole duty of man" (Ecclesiastes 12:13).*
- *"Many are the plans in the mind of a man, but it is the purpose of the Lord that will stand" (Proverbs 19:22).*
- *"All have sinned and fall short of the glory of God" (Romans 3:23).*
- *"For the wages of sin is death, but the free gift of God is eternal life in Christ Jesus our Lord" (Romans 6:23).*
- *"For God so loved the world, that He gave His only Son, that whoever believes in Him should not perish but have eternal life" (John 3:16).*
- *"If we confess our sins, He is faithful and just to forgive us our sins and to cleanse us from all unrighteousness" (1 John 1:19).*
- *"The people whom I formed for myself will declare my praise" (Isaiah 43:21).*
- ... *"your body is a temple of the Holy Spirit within you... (1 Corinthians 6:19a).*

- *"You are not your own, for you were bought with a price. So glorify God in your body" (1 Corinthians 6:20).*
- *"If anyone is in Christ, he is a new creation. The old has passed away, behold, the new has come" (2 Corinthians 5:17).*
- *"By this my Father is glorified, that you bear much fruit and so prove to be my disciples" (John 15:8).*
- *"Let everything that has breath praise the Lord! Praise the Lord!" (Psalm 150:6).*
- *And without faith it is impossible to please God because anyone who comes to Him must believe that He exists and that He rewards those who earnestly seek Him. (Hebrews 11:6)*
- *Let us fix our eyes on Jesus, the author and perfector of our faith, who for the joy set before Him endured the cross, scorning its shame, and sat down at the right hand of the throne of God. (Hebrews 12:2)*
- *This is the confidence we have in approaching God; that if we ask anything according to His will, He hears us. (1 John 5:14)*
- *And pray in the Spirit on all occasions with all kinds of prayers and requests. With this in mind, be alert and always keep on praying for all the saints. (Ephesians 6:18)*
- *A new command I give you: Love one another. As I have loved you, so you must love one another. By this all men will know that you are My disciples, if you love one another. (John 13:34-35)*
- *As a prisoner for the Lord, then, I urge you to live a life worthy of the calling you have received. Be completely humble and gentle; be patient, bearing with one another in love. (Ephesians 4:1-2)*
- *Do nothing out of selfish ambition or vain conceit, but in humility consider others better than yourselves. Each of you should look not only to your own interests but also to the interests of others. (Philippians 2:3-4)*
- *And the Lord's servant must not quarrel; instead, he must be kind to everyone, able to teach, not resentful. Those who oppose him he must gently instruct, in the hope that God will grant them repentance leading them to a knowledge of the truth. (2 Timothy 2:24-25)*
- *And let us consider how we may spur one another on toward love and good deeds. Let us not give up meeting together, as some are in the habit of doing, but let us encourage one another – and all the more as you see the Day approaching. (Hebrews 10:24-25)*

- *Live in peace with each other. And we urge you, brothers, warn those who are idle, encourage the timid, help the weak, be patient with everyone. (1 Thessalonians 5:13b-14)*
- *Be devoted to one another in brotherly love. Honor one another above yourselves. (Romans 12:10)*
- *Share with God's people who are in need. Practice hospitality. (Romans 12:13)*
- *In the same way, let your light shine before men, that they may see your good deeds and praise your Father in Heaven. (Matthew 5:16)*
- *Preach the Word; be prepared in season and out of season; correct, rebuke and encourage – with great patience and careful instruction. (2 Timothy 4:2)*
- *In everything set them an example by doing what is good. In your teaching show integrity, seriousness, and soundness of speech that cannot be condemned, so that those who oppose you may be ashamed because they have nothing bad to say about us. (Titus 2:7-8)*

Some longer passages:

- "…What is man that you are mindful of him…?" Psalm 8:3-6
- Sons of God through faith, Galatians 3:25-29
- Peace with God through faith, Romans 5:1-6, Romans 6:1-4

Appendix F

Additional Assessment Examples

The Objective (Objective numbers include designators K, S, D, and P, representing knowledge, skills, dispositions, and parents.)	Assessment Type	Measurement[97]
KNOWLEDGE Number K:1 Identify four or more attributes of God	One-on-one criterion-referenced interview (not all questions need be asked within one interview) What can you tell me about God? What have you learned about what God is like? Do you know a Bible verse or words from a song that tell us what God is like? Can you remember words within a song that reminds us of what God is like?	Use a criterion-referenced listing of God's attributes and other truths about God as taught during the elementary program (e.g., Trinity, good, Creator, Father, holy, faithful, God is in Heaven, mighty, merciful, He forgives, loves, cares, heals, knows, is everywhere, etc.) Mark the attributes mentioned during the interview. Assessment Benchmark: Objective met if student identifies four or more truths. Not all questions are needed once five attributes have been identified.

Number K:3 Recognize Jesus as the second person within the Trinity and explain His role in God's plan for men, women, boys, and girls	One-on-one criterion-referenced interview Who is Jesus? Why did God send Jesus?	Criterion: God's son, God (person within the Trinity), the truth, the Way, our Redeemer, etc. Criterion: Because God loves us, to die for our sins, save us, so we can better understand what God is like. (Remember to always base criterion on what has been taught!) Benchmark: At least two answers to each question
Number K:4 Identify the role of the Holy Spirit in the life of the believer.	One-on-one criterion-referenced interview Why did God send the Holy Spirit?	Criterion: Develop the criterion based upon what has been taught (e.g., to comfort us, help us understand God's Word, lead us, enable us to live our lives for Jesus, etc.) Benchmark: At least two answers to the question
Number K:7 Know the basic elements of a naturalistic and humanistic worldview	A matching activity for use during a regular class period	Create a one matching exercise. Column One: A. Christian, B. Humanistic, C. Naturalistic. Column Two: This column would randomly list 15 answers to worldview questions. The items would include at least one answer to each of the four worldview questions (reality, truth, humankind, value) for each of the three worldviews, plus two additional random answers. Benchmark: At least 10 correct answers

Number K:6	Pass out a 3x5 index card. Have the student write an answer to each question on the card. Once everyone has written an answer, have the students pass in the cards (no names on the cards). Once collected, have the students orally share answers. Ask the four basic questions related to a biblical worldview. (What is real? What is true? What is of value? What is the nature of humankind?)	Create a four-part list of the possible answers to each question (The truths that were taught). Tally how often the various answers were found within the cards as a whole. Benchmark: Rank order the responses according to frequency. Identify what was and was not remembered. (curriculum evaluation) Count the number of cards that had a correct answer to all four questions. Count the number of cards with three correct answers. What percentage of the class were found within each group?
Answer the four basic questions related to a biblical worldview		
DISPOSITIONS **Number D:2** Recognize and value their uniqueness as one created by God	**Interview**: One-on-One Interview Can you tell me some important things about yourself? What does God's Word say about who you are?	Record truths related to their being made in the image of God, their uniqueness, that they are designed for a purpose, ambassadors for Christ, etc. Benchmark for D:2: Identifies two or more Biblical truths
Number D:6 Value their talents and spiritual gifts and develop them as a means to glorify God.	Do you have a talent or spiritual gift? Are you using these abilities? If so, how?	Record talents or possible spiritual gifts. If provided, record a way in which they are using the gift. Benchmark D:6: Identifies a gift or talent and how it is being used.

Number D:5	Parent Survey (online)	Likert Scale responses, using a four-point scale. Average the four points earned.
Choose God's will and obedience over a desire to go one's own way	Does your child respond positively to going to church? Does your child evidence a desire to obey or apply God's Word? Does your child show respect for you and his or her grandparents?	**4: All the time** **3: Most of the time** **2. Sometimes** **1. Seldom** Assessment Benchmark Average score of 2.75 or above on the four questions.
Number D:4 Choose to demonstrate gratitude, kindness, generosity, empathy, forgiveness, and love to others.	**Ongoing Observations and Parent Questionnaire** Teacher: Note acts of gratitude, kindness, generosity, empathy, forgiveness, and love to others during class or other ministry-related activities (anecdotal record) This assessment could be ongoing during both fourth and fifth grade. Parent Questionnaire: Can you recall acts of kindness, generosity, care for others, and any other character traits that your child may have shown over the past few months? If so, please list up to three examples.	Award one point for each notation on the observation record. Award a point for each example cited by the parent up to four points. Combine the observation and questionnaire totals. **Assessment Benchmark:** A score of five or more points Score the record according to the number of times each student has accurately participated. **Additionally:** Tally the total number of times that each character trait was recorded. Rank order the traits and note a trait that may need more emphasis in order to more effectively impact the students.

Number S:2	Ongoing anecdotal record: Note each time a student accurately responds during a "worldview detective" or book club discussion.	Score the record according to the number of times each student has accurately participated. When having a discussion, have a volunteer monitor the participants and their responses.
Recognize or discern a non-biblical worldview when heard, viewed, or read.	• Accurately identifies a worldview clue during a discussion • Suggests the worldview of the author • Contrasts the worldview within what is read or viewed to that of a Christian	The number of responses needed to represent satisfaction of the objective should be based upon the frequency or number of opportunities (discussions) to participate. For example, the student has evidenced worldview thinking within at least three or more discussions
Number P:3 (Parents) Attend parent focus groups and other forms of parent education	An attendance record kept across the three years of upper elementary involvement	The percentage of times in attendance. **Assessment Benchmark:** Participated in a minimum of 50%

Appendix G

Using Literature to Advance Worldview Thinking

Additional Suggestions to Consider		
The Whipping Boy Sid Fleischman	A well-known classic story of a prince whose punishment is transferred to a pauper. Prince Brat and the whipping boy trade places after becoming involved with dangerous outlaws. A story of character transformations follows.	Grade three The nature of boys and girls Value Truth Questions: What is the root of the Prince's behavior? What changes him? What was different about the pauper? What was at the root of the changes in the boys?
The Hundred Dresses Eleanor Estes	Children bully and tease a classmate who wears the same dress each day because it is all she has. The children learn about empathy for the poor and not remaining silent when others are being tormented.	Grade three The nature of man Value (right and wrong) Questions: Why do the children treat their classmates the way they do? What brings about the change in their behavior?
Chicken Sunday Patricia Polacco	This is the story of relationships within a diverse community. The story centers around character—truthfulness, empathy, and care for others.	All grades The nature of man Value (character) Reality Questions: How did lying to the grandmother impact the children? Do you think the grandmother was a Christian? Why or why not?

Hatchet Boy Gary Paulson	This is a survival story. A boy stranded on an island after the crash of a small plane uses his determination, creativity, resourcefulness, and a hatchet that his dad had given him prior to his flight to survive months of isolation and hardship.	Grade five The nature of man Questions: How does this story demonstrate that we are created in the image of God? What was the worldview of the boy in the story? The worldview of the author?
Missing May Cynthia Rylant	When May dies, 12-year-old Summer, Uncle Ob, and Summer's friend, Cletus, band together to get her back—or at least hear from her as a means to help each other ease the pain from their loss.	Grade five Reality Questions: What worldview question were Summer and the other characters seeking answers to? What is the worldview of the author of this book?
The Return of the Twelves Pauline Clarke	A boy finds 12 old wooden soldiers hidden in the attic of a farmhouse his family has recently moved into. Through the boy's love for the soldiers, they become alive and seek to return to the famous people who had owned them over 100 years earlier. Their journey back home is reminiscent of the 12 tribes returning to the Promised Land.	Grade four or five Reality The nature of man Value Questions: What does this book reveal about the author's worldview? Does this story reflect any truths from the Bible? Who does Max represent? What can we learn about God from Max?
Number the Stars Lois Lowry	Through the eyes of 10-year-old Annemarie, readers witness the Danish Resistance's effort to smuggle the Jewish population of Denmark across the sea to Sweden. The heroism of an entire nation reveals human decency among the people during a dark period of history.	Grade four or five Nature of man Value (right and wrong, character) Questions: Why are people the way they are? What is the root of prejudice? How were the people of Denmark different? Why do you think they were different?

Junkyard Wonders Patricia Polacco	A preteen girl finds herself placed once again in a special ed classroom due to her dyslexia. The classroom is referred to as "The Junkyard," and the students are bullied and shunned by others. This true story follows the "power of one" from a teacher that convinces each child of their worth and ability.	All grades The nature of boys and girls Value Questions: What was so special about Mrs. Peterson? What biblical truths can be uncovered in this story? What have you learned about yourself as you listened to or read this story?
The Indian and the Cupboard Lynne Reid Banks	A young boy discovers that placing a toy Indian in a cupboard brings the toy to life. This book is a fun adventure story that discovers true friendship.	Grade four Nature of man Value Questions: Why do the Indian and cowboy not get along? How does Omri show love to the Indian? What sacrifice does Omri make at the end of the book? What would you do? Why?
The Best Christmas Pageant Ever Barbara Robinson	The Herdmans are every teacher's nightmare! But when they show up at the church and desire to be a part of the Christmas Pageant, chaos ensues!	Grade three Nature of man Reality Truth Value Questions: What behaviors do the Herdmans exhibit? How did the church people respond to the Herdmans? How did Imogene change? How did the main narrator change? What would you do if the Herdmans showed up at your church? Why would you react this way?
Little House in the Big Woods Laura Ingalls Wilder	Follow the Ingalls family as they have adventures in the big woods of Wisconsin. From wolves to bears to snow, Laura learns about the importance of family.	Grade three Nature of man Value Questions: How do the girls react to their Christmas gifts? In what ways do Ma and Pa show love to their girls?

The Lion, the Witch, and the Wardrobe C. S. Lewis	Entering an old wardrobe, four children find a new world where it is always winter and never spring. The White Witch dominates, but Aslan is on the move.	Grade four Nature of man Value (right/wrong) Truth Reality Questions: How does Edmund change after he meets Aslan? What characteristics do you see in Aslan that are similar to Jesus? Can you tell the worldview of this author? How can you tell?
Tuck Everlasting Natalie Babbitt	Winnie meets an interesting family when she runs away from her own. Her new friends are in danger, and there is a secret they are hiding.	Grade five or six Nature of man Value (character) Questions: What is the motivation of the man in the yellow suit? What decision does Winnie make? What would you do in her situation? Can you justify what you would do based upon God's Word?
Because of Winn-Dixie Kate DiCamillo	When a stray dog becomes Opal's new friend, adventures begin and even more friendships are created.	Grade five Value (character) Questions: Describe the relationship between Opal and her father. What does Opal realize about Otis? What other things does Opal learn that summer?
The Phantom Tollbooth Norton Juster	Milo is bored with school. But when a tollbooth shows up in his bedroom, his view of the world changes.	Grade four or five Nature of man Value (character) Questions: How does Milo's view of education change? How does Milo learn the importance of thinking?

The Outsiders S. E. Hinton	The Greasers and the Socs have never gotten along. When Johnny kills a Soc in a fight, he and Ponyboy run. *mild language	Grade six or seven Nature of man Value (right and wrong) Identity Questions: Describe how the Greasers and Socs are similar and different. What does Ponyboy realize about his perceptions? How does the community value Johnny and Ponyboy after the fire? Why did it take a horrible event to show that the Greasers were people of value? How do the different members of the gang handle death?
Brown Girl Dreaming Jacqueline Woodson	This autobiography of the author written in poetry form follows her early days through elementary school. *Author is in the LGBT community, but the topic is not discussed in the book *The church should be a safe place to ask and discuss hard questions.	Grade seven or eight Value Identity Questions: What behaviors does Jackie's mother exhibit when they travel from Ohio to South Carolina? Why? How does Jackie feel about her South Carolina family? What types of people does she meet in New York? What event takes place that causes Jackie to realize that family is more than immediate family members? What does Jackie realize about herself and her brother and sister? What is the worldview of the author?
Charlie and the Chocolate Factory Roald Dahl	Charlie comes from a poor family. He barely has enough money to scrape together for a chocolate bar that might win him a trip to Wonka's Chocolate Factory. What happens when he opens the chocolate bar?	Grade four Nature of man Value (right/wrong, character) Truth Questions: Describe the characteristics of each of the children who found a golden ticket. What consequences happened because of the poor behavior and attitudes? What did the Oompa-Loompas do after each "accident"? What type of person did Willy Wonka want to take over his factory?

Scan this page to view more resources for *Distinctively Christian.*

References

1 Additional Editor's Note: Every worldview is grounded in a story or narrative that seeks to "give meaning to the world". Neil Postman within his book *The End of Education* (New York: Alfred A. Knopf. 1995. p.7) presents the argument that unless the narrative being taught provides meaning, learning has no purpose. Postman, even though not writing from the perspective of a biblical worldview, believed that ultimately the "truth" or "measure" of a legitimate worldview lies in the degree to which its narrative provides a "sense of personal identity, a sense of community life, a basis for moral conduct, and explanations of that which cannot be known". It is the story of God's plan to restore what was lost in the garden, that has the power to not only satisfy Postman's criteria, but redeem lives and restore individuals to their true identify. God's grace is found throughout the Bible's narrative and the Gospel is both its summary and climax.

2 See page 162 for additional resources.

3 See Appendix A for a summary and comparison of Erikson, Piaget, Kohlberg and Fowler.

4 Fowler, James. 1992. *Christian Perspectives on Faith Development.* Chapter 1. In Asltey, Jerff and Francis, Leslie editors. Herefordeshire, England: Gracewing Fowler Right Books & Grand Rapids, Michigan: Eerdmans Publishing.

5 Barna, James, *Transforming Children into Spiritual Champions.* Grand Rapids: MI: Baker Books. 2003.

6 Ibid.

7 Child Development Institute. "Erikson's Stages of Social Emotional Development". Accessed May 3, 2018. https://childdevelopmentinfo.com/child-development/erickson/#.WutWoqQvxOM.

8 Simms, Eva. *The Child in the World: Embodiment, Time and Language in Early Childhood.* Detroit: Wayne State University Press. 2008. Simms references David Elkind's use of the term frame to refer to the child's understanding of regularly occurring sequential events. Frames, for example, might include a bedtime, classroom calendar or evening meal routine.

9 Armstrong, Thomas. "The Stages of Faith According to James Fowler." American Institute for Learning and Human Development. Accessed online. September 3, 2020. https://www.institute4learning.com/2020/06/12/the-stages-of-faith-according-to-james-w-fowler/

10 Barna, James, *Transforming Children into Spiritual Champions.* Grand Rapids: MI: Baker Books. 2003. p.58

11 Ibid. p.109

12 Ibid. p.110

13 Schaeffer, Francis. in Stonestreet, John & Kunkle, Brett. *A Practical Guide to Culture: Helping the Next Generation Navigate Today's World.* Colorado Springs: CO. David C. Cook. 2017. p. 49

14 Ibid. p.49-50

15 Ibid. p.50

16 Some resources to get you started. Retrieved on September 3, 2020
    https://ratiochristi.org/blog/apologetics-resources-for-middle-school-students/?gclid=CjwKCAjw
    qML6BRAHEiwAdquMnRCZXhrKH-Cn7uSvGnPptrXiy12z3YMR32W9RNPzv55uSx0VfDIm
    mhoCHUsQAvD_BwE
    https://resurgensconsulting.com/apologetics-for-tweens/
    https://www.faithgateway.com/are-your-kids-ready-for-apologetics/#.X1EHeeeSnIU

17 Ferris, Robert. *Intimate & True: Bible Truths in Simple Terms*. Bloomington: Indiana.
    Westbow Press. 2018.

18 DeYoung, Keven. *The Biggest Story*. Wheaton, Il: Crossway. 2015.

19 Gaebelein, Frank. Accessed on May 15, 2018. https://biblicalstudies.org.uk/pdf/grace-
    journal/03-3_27.pdf.

20 Garrick, Gene. *Introduction to Christian Philosophy Applied to the Christian School*. p. 55.

21 Publishing Team, ESV Bbile. Introductions to 1st and 2nd Timothy. English Standard
    Version. Reference Edition. Wheaton, Il: Crossway. 2001.

22 Ortberg, John. *Everybody's Normal Until You Get to Know Them*. Grand Rapids, MI.
    Zondervan. 2014.

23 McQuilkin, Robertson. Dr. McQuilkin, former president of Columbia International University,
    has authored numerous articles and books dealing with sanctification and the victorious life.
    The steps outlined here are based upon his writings and messages during CIU chapels.

24 Howse, Brandon P. "National Test Reveals Christian Students Lack and
    Christian Worldview". Accessed on May 15, 2018. http://k.b5z.net/i/u/2167316/f/
    Lecture_3_What_is_a_worldview_Bethel_Revised_1.pdf

25 Barna, James, *Transforming Children into Spiritual Champions*. Grand Rapids: MI: Baker
    Books. 2003

26 Stonestreet, John & Kunkle, Brett. *A Practical Guide to Culture: Helping the Next Generation
    Navigate Today's World*. Colorado Springs: CO. David C. Cook. 2017

27 Fakkema, Mark. *Christian Philosophy and its Educational Implications*. Chicago: NACS.
    1952. B.1.5

28 Ferris, Robert. *Intimate & True: Bible Truths in Simple Terms*. Bloomington: Indiana.
    Westbow Press. 2018. p. 13.

29   Moore, Russell. "How Do You Explain the Trinity to Children. Accessed
    online on November 16, 2018. https://www.russellmoore.com/2016/04/28/
    how-do-you-explain-the-trinity-to-children-2/

30 Ferris, Robert. *Intimate & True: Bible Truths in Simple Terms*. Bloomington: Indiana.
    WestBow Press. 2018. p.173.

31 Pantheism defined: "At its most general, pantheism may be understood positively as the view
    that God is identical with the cosmos, the view that there exists nothing which is outside of
    God, or else negatively as the rejection of any view that considers God as distinct from the
    universe" Stanford Encyclopedia of Philosophy. Accessed online on September 28, 2020.
    Pantheism is included as a worldview for discussion in that spiritualism is evident throughout
    contemporary culture and even expressed within some Disney movies.

32 Zuck, Roy B. and Clark, Robert E. editors. *Childhood Education in the Church*. Chicago: Moody. 1975.

33 Lewis, Sarah. *Worldviews: Children's Introduction to Missions*. Orlando, FL: Pioneers. 2018.

34 Garrick, Gene. *Introduction to Christian Philosophy Applied to the Christian School*. Norfolk, VA: Tabernacle Church of Norfolk. Unpublished manuscript. p.12.

35 ibid. p.24.

36 Ferris, Robert. *Intimate & True: Bible Truths in Simple Terms*. Bloomington: Indiana. WestBow Press. 2018. p.7.

37 Holmes, Arthur. *All Truth is God's Truth*. Grand Rapids, MI: Eerdmans Publishing Co.1977. p.32.

38 Garrick, Gene. *Introduction to Christian Philosophy Applied to the Christian School*. p.28.

39 Ferris, Robert. *Intimate & True: Bible Truths in Simple Terms*. Bloomington: Indiana. WestBow Press. 2018. p.8-9.

40 https://foundationworldview.com/. Elizabeth Urbanowicz's work should be considered as a primary resource for teaching worldview during the elementary school years. A sample lesson is available via the website.

41 Ibid. Unit 1, Lesson 1 in the foundation Worldview Curriculum "What is Truth".

42 www.newcitycatecism.com.

43 DLTK-Bible website. Accessed on January 5, 2019. http://www.dltk-bible.com/poems-bible.htm.

44 For the words to this hymn and the previous two go http://lnwhymns.com/HymnTopics. aspx?ID=80 Accessed on September 14, 2020.

45 Retreat Christian Ministries. "Spiritual Formation." Accessed on June 20, 2020. https://retreatchristianministries.com.au/our-vision/spiritual-formation/.

46 Garrick, Gene. *Introduction to Christian Philosophy Applied to the Christian School*. p.31.

47 Colson, Charles, Pearcy, Nancy. *The Christian in Today's Culture*. Wheaton Il: Tyndale House. 1999. p. 40.

48 Garrick, Gene. *Introduction to Christian Philosophy Applied to the Christian School*. Unpublished manuscript. p. 38.

49 Ibid. p. 23.

50 Ibid. p. 24.

51 Refer to Appendix A.

52 The Psychology Notes HQ. "Kolberg's Stages of Moral Development". Accessed on June 20, 2020. https://www.psychologynoteshq.com/kohlbergstheory.

53 Damon, William, *The Moral Child: Nurturing Children's Natural Moral Growth*. New Youk: Free Press. In Uecker, Milton. *Foundations of Christian School Education*. Colorado Springs: Purposeful Design. 2003. p. 229.

54 Ibid. p. 229.

55 Coles, Robert. *The Moral Intelligence of Children. New York:* Putnam. 1998. p.16.

56 James, Helen Foster. Media Services Coordinator. San Diego County Office of Education. Accessed online on June 20, 2020. https://ats.apsva.us/wp-content/uploads/legacy_assets/ats/e7c909cc71-character-traits-hfj.pdf

57 Washburn, Kevin and Julia. "Make Way for Books". Helena, Al. May/June 1996. pp 1-2.

58 Smith, Christian. *Soul Searching: The Religious and Spiritual Lives of American Teenagers*. New York: Oxford University Press. 2005.

59 Butler, J. Donald. *Four Philosophies and their Practice in Education and Religion*. 2nd ed. New York: Harper and Row. 1968. p. 558.

60 Childs, John L. *Education and Morals* (p. 57). In Garrick p. 13.

61 Garrick, Gene. *Introduction to Christian Philosophy Applied to the Christian School*. p.15.

62 Ibid. p.16.

63 Ferris, Robert. *Intimate & True: Bible Truths in Simple Terms*. Bloomington: Indiana. WestBow Press. 2018. p. 19.

64 Ibid. p. 19-21.

65 Dr. Hatch's courses and lectures are available through the Hatch Library collection at Columbia International University, Columbia, SC.

66 See page 162 for additional resources.

67 Wilhoit, James C. & Dettoni, John M. *Nurture That is Christian: Developmental Perspectives on Christian Education. p.153.*

68 Anderson, M and Johnson, T. *GIST: The Essence of Raising Life Ready Kids*. Colorado Springs, CO: Focus on the Family. 2019.

69 See page 162 for additional resources.

70 Smith, Christian. *Soul Searching: The Religious and Spiritual Lives of American Teenagers*. New York: Oxford University Press. 2005.

71 Warren, Rick. *God's Big Plans for Me: Storybook Bible*. Grand Rapids, MI: Zonderkidz. 2017. Stories are based on stories from Hurlbut's *The Complete Book of Bible Stories*. Edited by Jon Walker.

72 Hays. Edward L. "Evangelism of Children". Chicago: Moody. 1975. In Zuck, Roy B. and Robert E. Clark (editors). *Childhood Education in the Church*. Chapter 11. p.153 and 159.

73 Tripp, Ted. *Shepherding a Child's Heart*. Wapwallopen, Pa: Shepherd Press. 1995.

74 Postman, Neil. *The End of Education*. New York: Alfred A. Knopf. 1995.

75 Goldstone, Lawrence and Nancy. *Deconstructing Penguins*. New York: Random House. 2005.

76 Barna, James, *Transforming Children into Spiritual Champions*. Grand Rapids: MI: Baker Books. 2003. p. 67-70.

77 Stetzer, Ed. "Making Sure Children Actually Hear the Gospel and Not Just a Bunch of Bible Stories." Christianity Today. February 2015. Accessed on June 20, 2020. https://www.christianitytoday.com/edstetzer/2015/february/making-sure-children-actually-hear-gospel-and-not-just-bunc.html.

78 Browne. Chris. *Beyond the Walls: Equipping Students to Leave School Without Leaving Their Faith*. Wheaton, Il: Wheaton Press. 2012. p.41.

79 Ibid. p. 41.

80 Joy, Donald in Zuck and Clark editors. *Childhood Education in the Church*. Chicago: Moody. 1975. Chapter 1. p 19-20.

81 Browne. Chris. *Beyond the Walls: Equipping Students to Leave School Without Leaving Their Faith*. Wheaton, Il: Wheaton Press. 2012. p.41.

82 Hayes, Edward. *Childhood Education in the Church*. Chapter 11. p.159.

83 Spackman, Carl K. *Parents Passing on the Faith*. Wheaton, Il: Victor Books: Scripture Press. 1989, p. 76.

84 Piper. John. 1980 Sunday evening message to congregation. Accessed online on June 20, 2020. https://www.desiringgod.org/messages/the-children-the-church-and-the-chosen.

85 Headings or labels like mission, purpose, vision, objectives, standards and outcomes are often used interchangeably. For example, mission and purpose are sometimes thought to be the same thing as are labels like objectives and outcomes. A curriculum framework and its contents is a design specific to an educational context and application.

86 This mission of Ben Lippen School's primary (Pre-K through 2) unit. Columbia International University, Columbia, SC.

87 Life.Church NextGen. "Spiritual Growth Outcomes for NextGen Ministry Transition Points". Accessed online on September 8, 2020. https://open.life.church/items/155917-next-gen-spiritual-growth-outcomes-pdf

88 Ibid.

89 Wiersbe, Warren W. *The Wiersbe Bible Commentary*. Colorado Springs: CO. David C. Cook. 2007. p. 864.

90 Barna, George. *Transforming Children into Spiritual Champions: Why Children Should be Your Church's #1 priority*. Ventura, CA: Gospel Light. 2003.p.124.

91 Ibid. p.126.

92 This outcome can be developed into a series of attitudes or values that will be emphasized across grades three through five. The specific traits should be selected based upon the program's vision or those within a published curriculum.

93 http://www.ala.org/alsc/awardsgrants/bookmedia/newbery Accessed on October 12, 2020.

94 http://www.ala.org/awardsgrants/content/shiloh Accessed on October 12, 2020.

95 Ferris, Robert W.*Intimate & True: Bible Truths in Simple Terms*. Bloomington, IN: Westbow Press. 2018.

96 Information on John Piper's ministry. Accessed May 15, 2018. https://www.childrendesiringgod.org/documents/curriculum/scope/abc_expanded.pdf

97 Measurement involves the conversation of data into a number or statistic.

www.EngagedSchools.com

© 2021, The Engaged Schools Initiative

Made in the USA
Columbia, SC
04 September 2021